CIVIL WAR REGIMENTS

FROM

WISCONSIN

JEROME A. WATROUS

eBooksOnDisk.com
2003

Orginially Published in 1908
by the
Federal Publishing Company

CONTENTS

JEROME A. WATROUS

Lieut-Col Jerome A. Watrous, U. S. Army, was born in Conklin, Broome Co., N. Y., Sept. 6, 1840. When four years old his parents removed to Wisconsin. Four years later, his father Capt O J. Watrous, died, and his mother and her chil-dren returned to York state. The subject of this sketch worked on a farm for his board and clothes and three months of schooling each winter until he was fifteen. At sixteen he taught school one term in Pennsylvania, and in 1857 he returned to Calumet Co., Wis. He taught school the winters of 1858-59; attended Lawrence university part of a term, then began his career as a printer, and a few months later as an editor. He was an editor and publisher at Appleton when the Civil war broke out and he enlisted under President Lincoln's first call, but the company, like thirty others, was not ordered to camp. He again enlisted, under the next call, and was mustered in July 16, 1861, as a private of Co. E, 6th Wis. infantry. The following winter he was made ordnance-sergeant of a brigade, and after the battle of Antietam was advanced to ordnance-sergeant of a division. He reenlisted at the end of three years, was made sergeant-major of his regiment and a little later first lieutenant and adjutant, finishing his service as adjutant-general of the "Iron Brigade" on the staff of Gen. John A. Kellogg. His horse was shot under him at the battle of Gravelly run, Va., March 31, 1865, and he was captured and taken to Libby prison. For service in the last named battle he was brevetted captain. Upon muster out May 15, 1865, the young officer returned to his calling as an editor, first on the Jackson County Banner. In 1866 he was county superintendent of schools and that fall he was elected to the state legislature from the counties of Jackson and Clark. He declined a renomination and in 1869 became one of the editors and proprietors of the Fond du Lac Commonwealth, and was one of the founders of the present daily Commonwealth. In 1870 he was the Republican candidate for Congress for that district. In 1879 he be-came one of the editors and proprietors of the Milwaukee Telegraph, and for fifteen years was its editor, during which time he served as collector of customs for the Milwaukee district, and also as department commander of the Grand Army of the Republic. He served as colonel and later as brigadier-general on the staff of Gen. J. M. Rusk. At the opening of the Spanish-American war Gen. Watrous tendered his services to both the governor of the state and the president. June 15, 1898, he was commissioned a major in the regular army and served on the Atlantic coast until June, 1899, when he was made chief pay-master of the Department of the Columbia on the staff of Gen. W. R. Shatter, with headquarters at Portland, Ore. The following year he was assigned to duty at Manila. Six months later he was made chief paymaster, Department of the Visayas, and in Dec., 1901, when the four departments were consolidated into two, Maj. Watrous became chief paymaster, Department of the South Philippines, on the staff of Maj .-Gen. J. T. Wade. In Sept., 1904, he was promoted to lieutenant-colonel, U. S. army and retired for age. Since then he has followed his old calling as a writer and now resides at Whitewater, Wis. Col. Watrous is the associate-editor of this work for the state of Wisconsin. He has been a 33d degree Mason since 1888.

Wisconsin was intensely loyal. Her position at the extreme northern boundary of the country rendered her people less susceptible to the taint of treason, so pronounced in the states, nearer the border. Traitors there were; and others whose lack of force and of comprehension of conditions made them half-hearted sympathizers; but their numbers were small, their influence limited.

The various attempts to extend slavery, the scarce-concealed contempt of the South for the North, and the constant encroachments of the slave-power had stirred the wrath of the people of Wisconsin as well as elsewhere. One act was particularly repugnant—that known as the "Fugitive Slave Law"—and its application was bitterly resented. The arrest of the former slave, Glover, at Racine; his incarceration at Milwaukee, pending his delivery to his former master, by a United States commissioner; his sensational release by a mob headed by Sherman M. Booth, editor of the Milwaukee Free Democrat; and the arrest, escape, and subsequent arrest and conviction of the latter, aroused the people of the state to a pitch of excitement and anger well nigh inconceivable at the present time.

In effect the supreme court of the state held the fugitive slave law to be unconstitutional, and the people declared its enforcement an outrage. An application for a writ of habeas corpus made by Booth's attorney was granted, Justice A. D. Smith writing the opinion, which concurred in the claim of the application that Booth had been "unjustly restrained of his liberty; his detention was illegal because the fugitive slave act, under which he was committed, was unconstitutional." The supreme court afterwards—July 19, 1854—affirmed the decision, after considering an agreement on the writ of certiorari. Chief Justice Whiton, delivering the opinion, in closing said:

"The states—the free states—will never consent that a slave owner, his agent, or an officer of the United States, armed with process to arrest a fugitive from service, is clothed with entire immunity from state authority; to commit whatever crime or outrage against the laws of the state; that their own high pre-rogative, writ of habeas corpus, shall be annulled, their authority defied, their officers resisted, the process of their own courts contemned, their territory invaded by Federal force, the houses of their citizens searched, the sanctuary of their homes invaded, their streets and public places made the scene of tumultuous and armed violence, and State sovereignty succumb, paralyzed and aghast, before the process of an officer unknown to the constitution and irresponsible to its sanctions. At least, such shall not be the degradation of Wisconsin, without meeting as stern remonstrance and resistance as I may be able to interpose, so long, as her people impose upon me the duty of guarding their rights and liberties, and of maintaining the dignity and sovereignty of this State."

In passing, it may be noted that Booth was arrested the following day upon a warrant issued by Andrew G. Miller, Federal judge, a proslaveryite, and after the trial jury had failed to agree, Judge Miller practically instructed it to convict him on the ground that he had drawn up resolutions to the effect that "every person has an indefensible right to a fair and impartial trial by jury on all questions pertaining to his liberty," invoking the aid of habeas corpus, and pledging the efforts of all to a fair trial for Glover. The jury found him guilty of aiding Glover to escape, but acquitted him of resisting an officer. Judge Miller sentenced the prisoner on both charges, to pay a fine of $1,000 and costs amounting to $461.01, and to stand imprisoned until fine and costs were paid. This set the country on fire and indignation meetings were held in every large city, at which large sums of money were subscribed to pay the fine and costs. Booth was again released by the supreme court, which reaffirmed its power of habeas corpus issuances in cases of illegal imprisonment, and declared that without such power the state would be "stripped of one of the most essential attributes of sovereignty," and unable to "protect its citizens in the enjoyment of their personal liberty upon its own soil." The court refused the request for a writ of error to the United States supreme court, whereupon the latter tribunal made a requisition for the record and papers, threatening the clerk of the court with arrest and deportation from the state if he refused. He refused and the United States supreme court, having secured a certified copy of the proceedings, sent a remittur to the Wisconsin court to reverse its decision and remand Booth into Federal custody. This was refused, and so hearty was the approval of the press and people that the case was some years later made the basis of a charge that Wisconsin was as steeped in the doctrine of state rights and contempt for the government as any state in the Union. But as the charge, in the form of a pamphlet used for campaign purposes, was of a partisan nature, with no attempt at an analysis of the conditions prevailing, it fell of its own weight.

The case against Booth dragged its weary way through the courts in various phases for six years, he being reimprisoned in 1860 upon the judgment of five years before, although released originally by a writ of habeas corpus; his request for release being denied by U. S. Atty. Gen. Jeremiah S. Black. Only after his successor, Edwin M. Stanton, had pointed out to Buchanan the disastrous effects of Black's decision did the president grudgingly grant the pardon sought.

But the result of this remarkable controversy was to solidify a sentiment which had gradually formed in the northwest as a result of the Dred Scott decision, the Missouri Compromise and the Kansas-Nebraska bill, all serving to pave the way for the formation of a new party, destined to bring into line the scattered forces opposed to the states rights and pro-slavery contentions; and in Wisconsin the infant drew its first breath. When the Kansas-Nebraska bill was reported in Congress in the winter of 1853-54, Alvin E. Bovay, of Ripon, called a public meeting in that city on the evening of Feb. 28, 1854. It was there decided to organize a new party along the lines he suggested, with the non-extension of slavery as its most pronounced feature. At a subsequent meeting, held March 20, Mr. Bovay suggested the name "Republican" for the new party. The various parties were well represented at this meeting, and as a result the town committees of the Whig and Free-Soil parties in that place were dissolved and a committee of five chosen to act for the new organization. The outcome was a state con-vention, held in Madison July 13, following, at which a state organization was perfected and the name "Republican" adopted. A majority of the next delegation in Congress was elected by this new party, and Charles Durkee, a former Free-Soiler, was elected United States senator the following year, as a Republican. Mr. Bovay first approached Mr. Greeley with reference to the formation of a new party in 1852, while dining with him during the

5

convention which nominated Gen. Scott for the presidency. He predicted Scott's nomination and defeat, and declared that the impending campaign would be the last one for the Whigs as a national party. He proposed a new party and suggested the name "Republican." This suggestion he renewed when Greeley committed himself to the dissolution of the Whig party in 1854.

The first Republican governor of Wisconsin was Coles Bashford, elected by a small majority in 1855, counted out by over-zealous partisans through improvised sets of supplemental returns of election, but seated by the supreme court on incontrovertible evidence of his election. The same party gave the electoral vote of the state to Fremont in 1856, elected Alexander W. Randall governor in 1857 and again in 1859, building better than it realized.

Gov. Randall was an able, patriotic man, of deep convictions and decisive in action. In his message to the legislature in Jan., 1861, recognizing more fully than most men the gravity of the situation, he urged the necessity for prompt measures to put the state in readiness "to respond to the call of the national government for men and means to preserve the integrity of the union." "The signs of the times indicate that there may arise a contingency in the condition of the government, where it will become necessary to respond to a call of the national govern-ment * * * to thwart the designs of men engaged in an organized treason. * * * It is the part of wisdom to be prepared. The government must be sustained, the laws shall be enforced," he declared. Henceforth he made such preparations as lay in his power to prepare for the worst, believing that nothing could prevent war, and a few far-seeing men, including the editors of some of the leading papers of the state, rendered valuable assistance in preparing the minds of the people for the gathering storm. The State Journal of Jan. 4, 1861, declared that "civil strife seems inevitable. * * * There ought not to be less than 20,000 men, out of our 152,000 voters, armed and equipped;" and on the following day urged that the arming and equipping of the soldiers in the north ought to be begun at once. It voiced the sentiment of the state when, in its issue of March 4 it said:

"At 12 o'clock today the administration of James Buchanan ended. For eight years the country has struggled under uninterrupted misrule. These eight years of misrule leave what was the happiest, the most prosperous, the most contented nation of the earth, divided into hostile sections, its treasury exhausted, and its very existence involved in peril and doubt. * * * Thank God his term is ended, while there is still a nucleus left around which the patriotism of the people may rally with a hope of yet preserving the Union and restoring it to its pristine prosperity."

Notwithstanding the threatening signs, the people of the state had been so impressed with Lincoln's conciliatory inaugural address that the public mind was at ease. The news of Fort Sumter's fall was a shock, but it aroused every loyal citizen. Partisanship was forgotten. From every direction came offers of volunteers. Then it was that Gov. Randall displayed the real strength, the capacity, with which he was endowed.

The legislature, just about to adjourn sine die, was recalled and its adjournment resolution was rescinded. The measure, passed on the 13th, providing for the acceptance of volunteers, authorizing the uniforming and equipping of such volunteers, appropriating $100,000 for carrying out the provisions of the act and providing for the issuance of bonds for the amount, was declared insufficient by the governor in a brief message. The legislature promptly doubled the amount to be raised by bonds and passed an act exempting from civil process all persons enlisting and mustering for service. During the session some one struck up "The Star Spangled Banner," and in an instant the strain was taken up, not only in the senate and assembly chamber but by the clerks in the offices, and by scores who rushed to the building, the scene being one never forgotten by those who witnessed it. When the president's call for troops was received Gov. Randall at once issued his call. The response was instantaneous and overwhelming. In six days the 1st regiment was ready to go into rendezvous and every day brought offers of service from would-be volunteers. The governor requested repeatedly that Wisconsin's quota be increased.

At the beginning of the year the adjutant-general's report showed 130,000 men subject to military duty; fifty-two companies organized uniformed and armed, numbering 1,992 men; applications on file for organization and equipment of twelve more companies, which would have increased the number of state militia to 2,473.

Their armament was not of the best nor their work of a quality to commend them for instant service, but most of the members were patriotic and the organizations formed a nucleus for the work in hand. Several independent companies, which had taken pride in their work, tendered their services and were accepted. Eight of the ten companies composing the 1st regiment had attained some proficiency in drill which went far to lighten the burdens so suddenly placed upon the executive.

Company after company was organized and tendered the governor, despite the war department's declination of additional regiments. But Gov. Randall, realizing more clearly than many the magnitude of the contest, continued organizing and equip-ping troops, his military secretary having on the rolls enough companies for a dozen regiments. Contracts were immediately authorized for uniforms, shoes, caps, etc. Every effort was made to secure arms, but the government was unable to make immediate provision for them, and nothing suitable for the work in hand was obtainable. Camps were formed for the comfort of the regiments, suitable buildings erected, and the and, 3d and 4th regiments were ordered formed in advance of a call. Departments of quartermaster, commissary and paymaster were created; 1,600 army blankets were purchased in May, and thousands of yards of cloth were ordered from Wisconsin fac-tories. On May 7th word was received that all further enlistments must be for three years and on the 15th two regiments were called for. About this time the secretary of war wrote Gov. Randall that it was "important to reduce rather than enlarge the number" preparing for war. In the face of continued rebuffs of this nature, Gov. Randall kept his head and continued to organize and prepare regiments for the call he was certain would come.

The legislature was convened in special session on May 15. The governor, briefly narrating what had been done, asked for authority to at once equip and drill six regiments, and for an appropriation of $1,000,000. These requests were promptly complied with; the governor was authorized to keep two regiments in reserve at all times; to organize new ones as soon as those in rendezvous were called to the front; to transport, quarter, subsist, clothe and pay them while in camp, purchase military stores, field and camp equipage; to provide two assistant surgeons and necessary medicine for each regiment; to purchase 2,000 stands of arms; to employ such assistance as was necessary, and counties, towns, cities and villages were authorized to levy taxes for the maintenance of the families of volunteers.

The governor promptly organized efficient military departments the result of their work afterwards being made apparent by the excellent field work of the Wisconsin soldiers, their proficiency, and fine physical condition, as compared , with those from some other sections.

Through the strenuous efforts of Gov. Randall and Gen. Rufus King, the war department at last signified its willingness to accept six Wisconsin regiments instead of three, on the condition that they could be placed in readiness to move in three weeks. As a result, the 1st left the state June 9, the 2nd June 20, the 3d July 12, the 4th July 15, the 5th July 24, and the 6th on the 28th, all being in readiness at the appointed time. The defeat of the army at Bull Run opened the eyes of the secretary of war to the fact that the troops so freely offered were needed and the governor promptly assigned the necessary number of companies for the 7th and 8th regiments, but refrained from calling them into camp as long as possible, that the abundant harvest might be secured.

In the meantime the citizens had not been idle. The 1st regiment was full before the distant parts of the state knew of the call. The country's flag flew from every conceivable place. War meetings were held nightly. Hundreds volunteered their services. A great wave of patriotism swept over the state. In seven days after the issuance of the governor's proclamation, thirty-six companies had tendered service. Sympathizers with the South wisely kept silent— the spectacle of these quiet men of the Badger State throwing off their lethargy and casting themselves into the current that beat down all restraints was such as to inspire awe, dread and fear, and disloyalty dared not proclaim itself. The attack on Union troops at Baltimore April 19, intensified the feeling. At a meeting of the Milwaukee chamber of commerce on the 19th, with but one-half the members present, $11,175 was subscribed for the support of the families of volunteers. During the day the merchants of the city raised nearly

9

$9,000, and at another meeting of the chamber of commerce in the evening over $3,000 was subscribed. In addition many subscribed from $5 to $25 per month as long as the war continued, and in a few days Milwaukee had raised $30,000.

In Madison on the evening of the 18th $7,500 was raised for the same general purpose, and to this was subsequently added a considerable amount, Simeon Mills pledging $50 per month as long as the war should last. In Waupun a similar meeting secured some $3,000. Kenosha raised $3,543 in one hour at a meeting April 19. Fond du Lac's meeting produced some $4,000, Janesville secured over $5,300, Beloit $2,400, Clinton $2,500, Palmyra $1,500 and $5 additional for each volunteer. These are but samples of what was done all over the state. Some counties made a direct levy. Citizens pledged themselves to see that all needy families were cared for. The mayor of Oshkosh offered to equip a full company for the war.

In public meetings addresses were made which were inspiring and patriotic to the highest degree. Speaker Cobb, in bringing to a close the legislative session, said: "Though we may feel sad at heart, see that we show it not upon our faces. Let us meet this emergency * * * and master it as our forefathers met and mastered the troubles and dangers by which they were surrounded." On April 15 a public meeting was held at the capitol. Gov. Randall declared that Fort Sumter should be retaken and held and that whatever means should be placed at his disposal for equipping Wisconsin troops should be most faithfully employed in aiding to prosecute the war. Mayor Brown of Milwaukee said: "There is the flag of our country. He who can gaze upon it as it floats in the free air without a thrill of reverence or affection is a traitor. * * * That flag has waved over every battle-field that has secured liberty to our country; and wherever, in any part of the world, it has floated in the breeze, it has heralded to the nations civil and religious liberty." Matthew H. Carpenter stirred the crowd to wildest enthusiasm by his eloquent, finished address, of which only brief extracts are here given: "With everything to fill the hearts of the American people with thanks to God, and love toward each other, God has been forgotten, and brother is in arms against brother. * * * To quiet this unholy rebellion, to avenge this unendurable insult to our national flag, our people are rising as one man and every man feels insulted by this insult to his country. * * * Old, tottering Spain may now and then presume upon her imbecility, and slight our flag, and our careless and generous people will say with Berengaria, ' 'Tis but a silken banner neglected;' but when a whole state forgets her allegiance, when organized traitors levy war upon the national government and our national colors are lowered to the rags of treason, we all feel this is a stain upon our honor which no man has a right to forgive, and which the state must punish."

Senator James R. Doolittle, at the close of a remarkable arraignment of the Congress with which he had been associated, and of the leaders of secession, said: "I would hope and pray and labor still for a peaceful solution of this great national trouble: but if blood must flow, if it be His will that we must 'tread the winepress of the fierceness of his wrath' before we reach the end, be it so! In such a struggle, if true to ourselves, God the Almighty, must be with us."

At its convention at Madison Sept. 25, 1861, the Republican party adopted resolutions to the effect that the war "must be prosecuted for the sole purpose of suppressing treason and maintaining the constitution," and that the party "should not be confined in the present crisis to its own party in making nominations for office, but loyal and unconditional Union men of other parties are equally entitled to its confidence and support."

E. H. Brodhead, Democrat, was in favor of "taking the slaves of rebels, and using them in our army to perform labor, and, if thought best, to arm them." Jonathan E. Arnold, also a Democrat, would attack the enemy at every point and take their property, slaves and all. If necessary he would use the slaves as Jackson did the cotton—make ramparts of them and let the enemy destroy their property if they would.

The above quotations are from a few of the many addresses made from time to time at public meetings. From pulpit and press came stirring words to further arouse and maintain the spirit of patriotism which had taken possession of the people. While opposed in principle to the sword, the clergy of the state realized that here was a time corresponding to that which called forth from the Savior the declaration that He came "not to send peace, but the sword."

Rev. C. D. Helmer of Milwaukee, in a sermon a week after Sumter's fall, said: "It is vain to talk of holding back the popular mind from thinking upon this subject. Only dead men, and such as are as good as dead—I mean such as are morally, politically and patriotically fast asleep—will remain without a touch of excitement amid this national tumult." And again, with reference to slavery in its relation to the coming war and as an institution, he said; "Let the gates be opened and the sea of freedom begin to flow with extinguishing streams into the crater of oppression."

Rev. W. G. Miller of Milwaukee predicted a terrific struggle. "The war is inevitable. Its coming may be hastened or retarded by the shaping of events, but that civil war of a most frightful character is upon us is to my mind no longer a question. You can no more stay it than you can stay the leaping floods of Niagara. It is the legitimate offspring of an 'irresistible conflict' of ideas as antagonistic as light and darkness, as diametrically opposed to each other as right and wrong, truth and error. * * * The glove is thrown to us and we must accept it. If our principles are right, we would be unworthy of our noble pa-ternity if we were to shrink from the issue. The battle is for human liberty and it were better that every man should go down and every dollar be sacrificed, than that we should transmit to the coming millions of this land other than a legacy of freedom."

Rev. C. W. Camp of Sheboygan declared that "the Providence of God is summoning us to another work. We have looked back to the Revolution as our heroic age, and have hardly felt that the spirit of the fathers could be needed again. But we seem to be in a graver crisis now. All that they left us is in peril, and God and the interests of our children demand that we meet the peril bravely."

Rev. C. Collie of Delavan, said: "The fact that the war now forced upon us leads right in the direction of our true destiny, right in the line of work which God has given us to do, affords ground of hope that it is to be only an instrument to enable us to fulfill our heaven appointed service, and not a means of de-struction. * * * And if in this mad attempt (to fasten slavery upon the whole land) the South shall insist on an appeal to the issues of war, then God grant us a brave heart, good cannon, and a speedy victory."

Rev. W. W. Whitcomb: "It is God's war to purge away slavery. 'The Lord reigneth—let the earth rejoice.' "

These extracts might be multiplied by hundreds. But they serve to show the belief and the spirit of these "men of peace," many of whom, with a prayer-book in one hand and a musket in the other, went forth to fight the battles of the Union. Through all the troublous times that followed, the clergy of the state spoke and labored manfully for the success of the Union army, and so too did the press, which day by day sought to lift the drooping spirits of those who were left in the state to care for the weaker ones, the women and children, and to provide the "sinews of war."

To illustrate briefly the general attitude of the press of the state, a few extracts from leading papers are given herewith:

Daily Wisconsin, Milwaukee, April 13, 1861: "The rebels of Charleston have finally inaugurated civil war by commencing the bombardment of Fort Sumter. It is thus that the war is commenced against our country by the conspirators. We trust in God that the U.S. fleet will be able to relieve Maj. Anderson, and then give the South Carolina traitors such a lesson as will render their fate memorable in the history of great crimes."

On Apr. 15, the day the president's call for 75,000 men was issued, the Madison State Journal said: "We entreat the legislature to show no niggardly or stinting spirit in responding to the president's call. The people of the state will not justify it. The bill which is now in course of preparation should reflect the public spirit and loyal generosity of Wisconsin. If our porportion be only 1,500, let us treble or quadruple the number."

The Milwaukee Sentinel of Apr. 17 contains the following: "Animated by the infernal spirit which prompted the rebellion, the South has needlessly opened this war. Let this government now draw the sword and throw away the scabbard. Let us hear no more of peace till it comes in the appeal of trembling lips of conquered traitors. What may be the duration of this strife we cannot tell. How many lives, how much sacrifice of treasure it may involve, the future alone can reveal. But the man who doubts that the final result will be to crush out this treason and strengthen this government is weak of faith and judgment."

The Beloit Journal and Courier of April 18: "The Star Spangled Banner has been humbled and traitors have mockingly trodden its folds in the dust. A voice from every patriot's grave in the land demands that its honor be retrieved. Let the patriots of this day vow to redeem the proud old banner from dishonor. Our national existence, indeed, is once more at stake. No man with a true American heart in his breast, will fail to respond to the call of arms."

On April 18 the Waupun Times said: "Uncertainty has given place to reality—civil war has been inaugurated. The rebels have done an overt act—they have fired upon and captured, by force of arms a Federal fort, and there remains to the govern-ment no recourse but to maintain its rights and its power as a nation. There is no room for doubt and hesitation—men can no longer be Republican or Democrat—party is nowhere in this issue—every man must choose for himself between the proud title of patriot or the disgraceful name of traitor."

The La Crosse Union and Democrat: "There is a grand old storm arising—there will be such fighting as this country has never yet seen, and that right soon. This is no time for wavering. The Star Spangled Banner forever! Under its sacred shadow its forefathers fought and watched all through oppression's dark night. On its fair field of white, fair fingers toiled early and late, wrapped in its honored folds too many a brave and gallant man has gone to an honored grave, for it to be de-serted now. Wherever it floats, let America's sons gather, regardless of past differences, let it be protected with the blood of patriotic men, and may our arms seek not for rest until every insult given it be punished."

The Madison Patriot: "Now that war has begun, take our advice and push it to its bitter end. Let nothing be left undone. Strike your blows thick and fast and leave nothing to chance. The only parties we know are Unionists and disunionists. We belong to the former, thank God, and all who stand by us in that belong to 'our party.' All others are not only enemies of our common country, but our enemies."

The Fond du Lac Commonwealth: "If we must fight to maintain the authority of the nation, to keep it from tumbling into anarchy, and from being swayed by the meanest oligarchs that ever drew a blade for despotism, then let liberty blaze brightly upon our banners; and if the falchion for freedom must glitter in the sunlight, when it falls let tyrants feel the blow."

The Dodge County Citizen: "The government must be sustained. It is the cause of justice and truth. It is the cause of God. Popular liberty, for this and future generations, on this and other continents, must stand or fall by the constitution of these United States. Let the war come. Let every man do his duty and may God defend the right."

Departing from the policy of using infantry only, it was decided to form cavalry and artillery regiments, and in June Edward Daniels was given a special permit to raise a squadron of cavalry. This he did, and it proved a valuable adjunct and a credit to the state. About the same time a company of sharpshooters was recruited to form a part of Berdan's famous regiment, and left the state Sept. 23, the finest body of marksmen sent out from Wisconsin, and destined to perform gallant work.

On July 26, G. Von Deutsch was commissioned to raise a company of cavalry, which was speedily accomplished, the company joining Fremont's forces in September.

A message was received from the seretary of war on Aug. 13, requesting that all the available force in the state be sent to Gen. Fremont, together with "a full supply of field artillery and small arms." As the state had but six old, 6-pounder cannon, without caissons or harness, no arsenal or means of getting possession of guns, and possessing none except the 1,600 stands of arms antiquated and worn out by years of drill work, the seeming hopelessness of the task is apparent. Nevertheless, the 7th regiment was called into camp, its numbers coming from harvest fields, and the 9th, the German regiment was called into being. On the 19th a request was made for Wisconsin's home guards if they could be spared. To this the governor replied that the state had no home guards, but that if the gov-ernment would call for four, or six, or more regiments, agree to muster them into service at once, and to refund expenses on presentation of vouchers, the men would be forthcoming, and that a regiment of cavalry would be raised on the same understanding, as well as men for the artillery service. This brought a speedy order for five regiments and five batteries, and an offer of all the cannon, as well as such other arms, as might be required. The work of organization was rushed, commissions being issued the same day for raising companies of artillery. Sec. Cameron, in a subsequent communication said: "Permit me to extend the acknowledgments of this department for your prompt and liberal response to all calls that have been made upon you for forces." On Aug. 22, the first regiment was mustered out, its time having expired, but it was reorganized on the agreement of the war department to accept it. The 8th, 9th, 10th and 11th were speedily organized and ordered into camp; the 7th left the state, Sept. 21, and the 8th on Oct. 12.

Up to and including the 8th, the regiments had been clothed in grey, but the enemy having adopted that color, the result was confusion and uncertainty in battle, especially in "hand-to-hand" fighting. The government ordered blue to be substituted and this was carried out, the soldiers in many cases being compelled to pay for both suits without being reimbursed for the cast-off suit of grey.

Seven batteries were raised instead of five, and Fritz Anneke was appointed colonel. After much correspondence the additional two were accepted, but guns and supplies were not forthcoming.

A request for reimbursement for supplies and subsistence of the first six regiments amounting to $512,000, was met by the payment of but forty per cent of the amount.

Military Secretary Watson was sent to Washington early in October to ascertain what attention would be paid to the governor's request for equipment. He secured an order for 5,000 stands of arms and accouterments and the promise of horses for the artillery, if the state would furnish cannon. Also an order for organization of three additional batteries, five regiments of infantry, and six companies of cavalry in addition to the six already organized by Daniels. On Oct. 15, the governor telegraphed to the secretary of war that "unless steps were taken immediately to reimburse the state to some extent, he must stop and disband regiments and companies." This brought prompt reply that the disbursing officer would soon have the funds to pay all accounts. An application made by C. C. Washburn to raise a second regiment of cavalry brought a favorable reply from Washington,

On Oct. 25 the companies for the 12th regiment were called into camp and about the same time the 13th was called for. The reorganized 1st regiment was ordered away on the 28th, the 10th on Nov. 9, and the 11th on Nov. 20, the latter being the last regiment to leave the state in 1861.

Ex-Gov. Barstow, with the sanction of the war department, had engaged in the meantime in the organization of the 3d cavalry, and though ordered to discontinue early in November was soon permitted to proceed with it.

In early November the 14th was ordered organized, also the 15th (Scandinavian) and 16th. The 17th (Irish) was authorized and recruited during December and January, as was also the 18th, the last named completing the quota of infantry called for during Gov. Randall's administration. On Nov. 27 two of the artillery companies were ordered sent to Baltimore.

A general order was promulgated Dec, 3, ordering the recruiting service taken out of the hands of the state executives and placed with the general government, the result being the discontinuance of recruiting for some time, the government still seeming to cherish the delusion that the war was of a few months duration only. Co. K of the 2nd regiment was detached in December as a heavy artillery company, and a company under Capt. Stahel was sent late in December to take its place.

Gov. Randall's term of office expired Jan. 6, 1862, and he retired from office after a strenuous year's work, having accomplished an almost herculean task—that of placing the state on a war footing and keeping it up to the demands made upon it, under conditions that would have broken the spirit of a weaker man. Commencing without means, without military knowledge, or instructions from the government, he threw into the work all his tremendous energies and capacity. Offices made necessary were created and filled with capable men, state bonds disposed of and funds raised, regiment after regiment organized, clothed, fed and cared for, and without in any degree reflecting upon his successors, he left the impress of his work upon the state's military operations for lasting good. He retired only to be called upon to fill the post of minister to Rome. In 1863 he was appointed assistant-postmaster-general, and upon the resignation of Postmaster-general William Dennison in 1865, was appointed his successor. He died at Elmira, N. Y., July-26, 1872.

The selection of a military staff seems to have been a happy one. Adjt.-Gen. W. L. Utley, Q. M. Gen. Treadway, Com.-Gen. Wadsworth, Paymaster Gen. Mills and Surg.-Gen. Wolcott were men of ability and of incalculable aid to their chief. Private and Military Sec., W. H. Watson, brought to his work a clear brain and tireless energy. State secretary, L. P. Harvey, and state treasurer, S. D. Hastings, whose duties were more than doubled, were unusually capable men, and the election of the former as governor and the re-election of the latter as treasurer to succeed himself were significant of the estimate of the people as to their qualifications.

Though death brought Gov. Harvey's administration to a speedy close, he exhibited many qualities of executive ability in the few weeks covering the span of his official life. He reappointed all his predecessor's military staff, with the exception of adjutant-general, Augustus Gaylord being appointed to that position and retaining it until the close of the war. The government having assumed the work of recruiting, Maj. R. S. Smith entered upon his duties as superintendent of that service, and all that was left for the quartermaster, commissary and paymaster-generals to do was to settle up the business of their offices, which was accomplished during the summer and the offices were abolished.

In his message to the new legislature, Jan. 8, 1862, Gov. Harvey reported the war fund receipts to have been $957,368.79, of which amount there was on hand Jan. 1, a balance of $50,227.09. The state's total war expense to that date amounted to $1,656,659.98.

Upon his recommendations the legislature during the session, passed several acts with special reference to the military depart-ment of the state. One of these defined the rights of families; others fixed penalties for the issue of false papers; imposed duties on military officers in the field to make certain reports; suspended the sale of lands mortgaged to the state or held by the volunteer; authorized the issue of bonds for war purposes to the amount of $200,000; defined the duties of allotment commissioners; and authorized the appointment of surgeons to batteries and assistant-surgeons to cavalry regiments.

Some trouble was experienced by Gov. Harvey, as well as by his predecessor, in securing a settlement of the state's claims for money advanced for subsistence and payment of the troops, but after several months time over $300,000 was paid, leaving a few claims unsettled, which were laid aside because of irregularities for further consideration.

An order was received discontinuing recruiting after Apr. 3, the war department still retaining the hallucination that the army was strong enough to cope with the rebellion, but this order was annulled June 6.

On receipt of the news of the battle of Shiloh, knowing that several Wisconsin regiments were in that engagement, Gov. Harvey gathered supplies and necessaries for the wounded and sick and started for the scene with Surg.-Gen. Wolcott and a staff of medical assistants, calling en route at Mound City, Paducah and Savannah, where many of the wounded were in hospital. The wants of all were supplied, and the party prepared to return home.

On Saturday evening, April 19, the party was on board the steamer *Dunleith* at Pittsburg landing, awaiting the arrival of the steamer *Minnehaha*. The latter reached there about 10 o'clock and as it came alongside the *Dunleith* the governor, who was standing near the guards of the *Dunleith*, made a false step and fell overboard between the two boats. Dr. Clark jumped into the river, caught the wheel of the *Minnehaha* and reached for the governor, but missed him. Gov. Harvey was swept down stream and passed under a flatboat. The darkness of the night and the disaster being wholly unexpected all efforts to rescue the governor proved unavailing. The body was found April 27 about 60 miles below Savannah, and was sent home. At Chicago, as the funeral cortege passed along the streets, the bells of the city were tolled and the flag on the city hall was placed at half-mast. Upon arriving at Madison the body was conveyed to the assembly chamber, where it lay in state for 24 hours, with a military guard of honor stationed at the bier. The procession to the grave was one of the most notable ever witnessed in the state, including in its number a military detachment from the 19th regiment, state officers as pall-bearers, the United States officers, many members of the senate and assembly, judges, societies, members of the bar, and citizens of every rank, business and profession. Gov. Harvey's remains rest near the center of beautiful Forest Hill cemetery, at Madison. Although but 41 years of age, he had reached heights beyond those attained by most men of more mature years. Successively teacher, editor, business man, member of the first constitutional convention, state senator, secretary of state, and governor, he performed well the duties of each position and had won the confidence of the people, when death brought to an end the life so full of promise.

Lieut.-Gov. Salomon at once entered upon the duties of the office and proceeded to the organization of the 20th regiment, a call having been made for more troops. The regiment was in readiness Aug. 23, and a week later was sent south.

The legislature met June 3, having adjourned to that date in April. The governor reported in his message that with 24,000 men sent from the state, the executive was embarrassed in caring for the sick and wounded, by reason of no adequate measures having been taken by the legislature. An act was at once passed appropriating $20,000 for the purpose indicated.

On April 20 about 900 prisoners from the south were quartered at Camp Randall, remaining until the latter part of May, when they were sent to Camp Douglas, Chicago, and the 19th regiment, which had guarded them was sent to Virginia.

About this time Gov. Salomon united with the governors of the loyal states in a memorial to the president, urging that a large force be called into the field without delay to crush out the rebellion. The response was the call for 300,000 men, Wisconsin's quota being five regiments. The regiments were promptly called for, camps assigned at Oshkosh, Milwaukee, Racine, Madison and La Crosse and recruits offered one month's pay, and $25 of the $100 state bounty, in advance. Circumstances afterwards compelled the abandonment of state bounty. The regiments were filled up rapidly and as fast as organized left the state for the front. Gen. Sigel having been authorized by the government to raise twelve regiments, called upon Gov. Salomon for one, the Germans of the state speedily filled its ranks and the 26th left the state Oct. 6. The governor called for seven more regiments, all of which were in the field by April 1, 1863.

An extra session of the legislature was called for Sept. 10, the governor deeming it best to in some measure forestall the operations of the draft, which had been ordered. He recommended an "organization of the militia of the state, an enrollment of all able-bodied men between the ages of 18 and 45 years, to enable the state to respond promptly to any call which might be made, and, in case of draft, to make such exemptions as would cause the draft to fall lightly on those who would be distressed by its operations," recommending that those between 18 and 35 be called first and that class exhausted before the older men were called out. This recommendation was not heeded and the disgraceful draft riots followed. A state tax of $275,000 was ordered levied for the war fund to be used in the payment of warrants for state aid to families of volunteers; commissioned officers out of the state were authorized to administer oaths and take acknowledgments; soldiers in the field were given the right of suffrage; and counties, towns, cities and incorporated villages were authorized to raise money for bounties.

Under the draft for 300,000 nine-months men, ordered Aug. 5, Wisconsin's quota was 11,904, and Gov. Salomon made the first and only draft made by the state authorities. By determined, repeated efforts he succeeded in getting an extension of recruiting time and the suspension of the draft from Aug. 15 to Nov. 10, and recruiting to fill old regiments was extended, bounty and advance pay to be continued. The war department had also failed to credit the state with the number of men actually furnished, having to its credit only 22,263 up to July 1, a surplus of only 510 to be applied on the state's quota under all calls. The state had actually furnished 24,653, making a surplus of 2,900 men, and after some correspondence this was credited. Unfortunately, volunteering in the new regiments was cut off in August, a grave error as it seems at this time, as the state's quota could have been filled without the application of the draft, the harvest being about completed and many being willing to enlist under the bounty and advance pay system.

At Milwaukee, in the make-up of the rolls, grave errors, to speak mildly, were made, and where that city's quota was properly over 700, the returns on their face showed but 105. The draft was postponed until the 19th, the rolls corrected, and with militia posted at every point, the draft was made without demonstration. In Ozaukee county a mob seized and destroyed the rolls, attacked several citizens and destroyed their property. The commissioner, a Mr. Pors, was thrown down the steps of the court-house and severely injured. He escaped with his life by hiding in a cellar and the interior of his handsome home was completely wrecked. Subsequently 130 of the rioters were arrested and imprisoned, the legislature settled for property destroyed and the state was afterward reimbursed by the government.

Riots at Port Washington made it necessary to send eight companies to that point. At Westbend a mob drove the draft commissioner out of town and broke up the draft. Four companies of militia restored and kept the peace at that place. Altogether 4,537 were drafted for the service, 1,739 were mustered in, 988 discharged, 19 deserted, 129 were furloughed, and 1,662 failed to report. At the close of the year 1862 there were three incomplete regiments in the state—the 27th and 31st volunteers, and 34th drafted. Their ranks were filled and all were in service by March, 1863.

When the legislature convened in Jan., 1863, the governor in his message reported the war fund as showing total receipts of $807,928.07 for the year and disbursements of $760,929.72. There was still due the sum of $105,803.48. He also reported that the enrollment showed 127,894 men liable to military duty, the state having furnished 38,511 men in the organization of new regiments, 2,155 recruits for old regiments, and 795 drafted men in camp. Total loss by deaths, discharges and desertion, 7,875.

Numerous acts of a military nature were passed; bonds to the amount of $300,000 were authorized for war purposes; a levy of $200,000 for aid to volunteers' families authorized; the soldiers granted the right to vote for county, circuit and supreme court judges; a special act establishing the process of commencing and prosecuting suits against those in the military service: amending the act suspending the sale of lands mortgaged to the state, or held by volunteers, extending the time to May 30, 1863; appropriating $15,000 for the care of sick and wounded soldiers; giving volunteers the right to redeem lands sold for taxes within two years from April 1, 1863;

extending the volunteer aid to families for six months after the death of the soldier; special bounty acts, and numerous minor ones.

No additional regiments were organized during 1863, the old ones being furnished with recruits. The 13th light battery was organized this year, but did not leave until Jan. 28, 1864. Cos. B, C and D, heavy artillery, were also recruited and sent forward, with Co. A as a base, the intention being to form a battalion. The conscription act was put into force Nov. 9. The enrollment numbered 121,202 and included all males between 20 and 45 years of age, divided into two classes. The first was composed of those between 20 and 35 years and all unmarried men subject to military duty between 35 and 45 years. From their numbers was to be made a draft of one-fifth the number enrolled with 50 per cent added. From the enrollment of 121,202 the draft called for 14,935. Of the number 5,081 paid commutation, 2,689 failed to report, 6,285 were discharged, 252 furnished substitutes, and 628 mustered in person.

A call for volunteers, made Oct. 17, gave the state's quota as 10,281. In making the district assignments care was exercised by Adjt.-Gen. Gaylord to give credits by towns and wards of volunteers enlisted, much injustice having been done in drafting by the failure of the provost marshal-general to give credit when making the assignments of quotas. Bounties of $402 were offered to veterans and $302 to new recruits. Premiums were also offered to persons bringing in recruits. The war department was given assurance of exempton from the general draft ordered for January in such states as should fill their quotas by volunteers and every effort was made to induce men to voluntarily offer their services. The city of Madison led with an offer of $200 extra bounty to each volunteer and its quota was filled in a week. Other communities adopted this plan and the work progressed rapidly.

Gov. Salomon's term of office expired in Jan., 1864, and he gave way to his successor. Called into office under unusual conditions, through an unforeseen accident, he sustained well the reputation given the state by his predecessors. Whether engaged in the organization of regiments, the care of the suffering in the field, the carrying on of the detested draft against his personal wishes, or in conducting the affairs of the state, he acted with energy, good judgment and tact, his mental poise holding him above the wiles of partisans or political intriguers and giving to the administration a character and standing unsurpassed by any during those stormy days.

Gov. James T. Lewis was inducted into office on the first Monday in Jan., 1864, Wyman Spooner being lieutenant governor, and Lucius Fairchild, secretary of state. S. D. Hastings succeeded himself as treasurer for his fourth term; Winfield Smith, attorney-general; J. L. Pickard, state superintendent for the third time; and William H. Ramsey bank comptroller for a second term. Augustus Gaylord was reappointed adjutant-general; S. Nye Gibbs, assistant adjutant-general; N. F. Lund, quartermaster and commissary-general and chief of ordnance; E. B. Wolcott, surgeon-general; Frank H. Firmin, military secretary.

When the legislature met on the 13th Gov. Lewis reported in his message thirty-four regiments of infantry, three regiments and one company of cavalry, twelve batteries of light artillery, three batteries of heavy artillery, and one company of sharpshooters sent from Wisconsin, exclusive of three months men, an aggregate of 41,775 men, of which number 16,963 had been lost to the service by death, discharge and desertion. The amount received into the war fund during the year, including the balance at the commencement of the year, was $818,032.44. The disbursements amounted to $786,892.85. For sick and wounded $13,999.91 had been disbursed. The state's indebtedness was $1,775,000, the greater portion being for war purposes and chargeable against the general government. The amount paid to families of volunteers from the commencement of the war was $1,197,044.70.

The legislature authorized towns, cities and villages to raise money by taxation for the payment of bounties; amended the laws relating to extra pay for soldiers in the service, providing for relief of families, etc., that the unintentional discrimination be obviated; provided for the entertainment of returning regiments; repealed the allotment commissioners act; made the law relative to the sale of lands apply to drafted men as well as volunteers; levied a tax of $200,000 for aid of families; appropriated $10,000 for relief of sick and wounded; and authorized the borrowing of $650,000 for war purposes.

Under the bounty system the recruiting for new and old regiments progressed so rapidly that no draft was necessary for either the January call or the subsequent calls of Feb. 1 and March 14, those drawn by draft in November being credited to the proper localities in the last two calls The old regiments were fully recruited and three more regiments authorized. The government having authorized the reenlistment of men whose first term of service had not expired in the old regiments, as veterans, giving the regiment the right to the title of "veteran regiment," with 30 days furlough, on consideration of three-fourths reenlisting, three-fourths of the 3d reenlisted in Dec., 1863, and came home, being the first veteran regiment that received this furlough.

During 1864, besides the 100-day troops, the term of the three-years' service of non-veterans expired in the first twelve regiments of infantry, 1st and 4th regiments and one company of cavalry, Co. G, Berdan's sharpshooters, the first ten batteries of light artillery and battery A, heavy artillery. The 3d, 6th, 7th, 8th, 9th, 11th, 12th, 13th and 14th infantry, 4th cavalry and 7th light artillery, constituted veteran organizations by reenlistment. On April 8 veteran regiments on furlough received orders to join their brigades without a moment's delay, at the expiration of their leave.

In June, Gov. Lewis organized the 39th, 40th and 41st infantry regiments as 100-day men. On July 18 word was received that the state's quota under the call of that date for 500,000 volunteers was 19,032. Investigation showed that the enrollment lists had not been corrected, the names of men already furnished not having been stricken off, and the names of aliens and those physically disabled, still remaining on the lists. A corrected list being ordered, it was found that the quota was but 15,341. While investigating this, Adjt.-Gen. Gaylord also discovered that the excess of 4,352, found to be due the state in the settlement with the war department the previous October had never been credited, and this brought the quota down to less than 11,000.

Volunteers not coming forward rapidly enough a draft was made Sept. 19th, the number drawn being 17,534, of which number 2,494 were mustered in, 945 furnished substitutes, 6,724 were discharged, 7,367 failed to report, and 4 paid commutation. In 1865

Brig.-Gen. Lund, for so long the capable quartermaster-general, resigned, and James M. Lynch was appointed. Gov. Lewis' message to the legislature of 1865 showed that Wisconsin had furnished 75,133 men, with the further addition of three regiments of 100-day men. The amount of state indebtedness was $2,005,000, all for war purposes (excepting the $100,000 used for the erection of the state capitol) and properly chargeable to the general government. The usual necessary enactments were made by the legislature for military purposes, including the authorization of a loan of $850,000.

Under the call of Dec. 19, for more troops, the state's quota had been placed at 17,800. As usual it was found to be an error, Wisconsin having always furnished more than her share, and the number was reduced to 12,356. On April 10, 1865, Gov. Lewis formally notified the legislature of the surrender of Lee, saying: "Four years ago, on the day fixed for adjournment, the sad news of the fall of Fort Sumter was transmitted to the legisture. Today, thank God, and next to Him the brave officers and soldiers of our army and navy, I am permitted to transmit to you the official intelligence, just received, of the surrender of Gen. Lee and his army—the last prop of the rebellion. Let us rejoice and thank the Ruler of the Universe for victory, and the prospect of an honorable peace."

Gov. Lewis was a worthy prototype of those who had held the reins in the earlier days of the war. Popular he must have been, receiving every vote cast in his home town of Columbus when a candidate for secretary of state, and receiving a majority of 25,000 in the state when a candidate for governor. During his term over 38,000 troops were raised, the sick well cared for, the interests of the state carefully guarded, its credits secured, quotas corrected, the draft evils mitigated, and the people at home given every possible consideration.

It is but just to say in conclusion, that one of the most capable aids in military operations in the state was Adjt.-Gen. Gaylord. With duties unusually arduous, the department became one of the most important in the state at a time when any position involved transactions of great moment, imposing burdens unknown in the history of the state up to that time. Through it all with a multitude of detail, constantly increasing with the years, Gen. Gaylord kept his head, his well trained mind grasping the most intricate point, solving every problem, and preserving an almost perfectly organized system throughout, when it seemed as though chaos ruled at Washington.

This recognition of his services in no wise detracts from those of others equally faithful, and Wisconsin seems to have been fortunate in the possession of officials well qualified for their positions.

With that keen foresight which marked his every act, Gov. Randall realized the necessity of caring for the sick and wounded. He appointed Dr. E. B. Wolcott, of Milwaukee, surgeon-general of the state, April 17, 1861, and from that time until the close of the war Dr. Wolcott superintended the medical department of Wisconsin. Formerly surgeon of the U. S. army, he knew the requirements and provided surgical appliances, medical supplies and invalids' stores for the regimental surgeons and their assistants, and visited many a hospital and battlefield in person to see that everything was done that could be. Two assistant surgeons were appointed to each regiment and paid by the state.

On July 4, 1861, Gov. Randall addressed a letter to the governors of the loyal states, in which he called attention to the lack of care for the soldiers from the time they left their respective states, and urged united action that none might suffer unnecessarily in camp, field or hospital, or that the disabled ones be not left to find their way home, afoot and friendless. Agents were appointed to accompany the earlier regiments to the field and to attend to the distribution of supplies. Dr. Wolcott exercised such unremitting care that it came to be recognized that Wisconsin regiments were as well supplied as any, and better than many, of those of other states.

The governor was in New York when the battle of Bull Run occured. Hurrying to the scene, he employed several to look after the sick and wounded, relieving hunger and suffering and furnishing needed clothing.

An extra expenditure fund of $10,000 having been placed at his disposal May 25, 1861, the governor used it for alleviating conditions by engaging men to cook for and attend to the wants of the sick at Elmira, Harrisburg and other points, doubtless saving many lives. Other states adopted the idea, and the secretary of war complimented Wisconsin for adopting the system. Gov. Randall did not approve of "the policy of experimenting with soldiers to ascertain how little they could live on or how extreme privations they could endure and escape sickness or death."

Gov. Harvey was equally solicitous and it was while on an errand of mercy that he lost his life. Within 24 hours of the receipt of the news of the battle of Pittsburg landing, he with Dr. Wolcott and a staff of assistants, accompanied by Gen. E. H. Brodhead of Milwaukee, was on the way with supplies of every kind. Over 200 were found at Savannah alone, suffering from neglect. They were promptly cared for, the regiments within reach were visited and their needs supplied.

Gov. Salomon continued in the same manner to carry relief and see that everything was done of which the limited means at his disposal permitted. Invalid soldiers were brought home, and Surg.-Gen. Wolcott and Com.-Gen. Wadsworth, with assistants, visited the army before Corinth, where many were sick, provided proper care and greatly improved their condition.

The legislature appropriated $20,000 for the work in 1863, and Dr. Wolcott was authorized to visit the battlefields and hospitals to attend the sick and wounded. State agents were located at the principal military points east and west with excellent results. Regular information was furnished of the condition of those in hospitals, their needs supplied, many abuses remedied, and so far as possible they aided in securing the discharge of those unfit for service. Expeditions, headed by Dr. Wolcott, visited the battle fields at Perryville and Stone's river.

In his message to the legislature in 1863 the governor reported an expenditure of $10,828.94 and a further appropriation of $15,000 was made for the work.

From the beginning of his term Gov. Salomon and others had labored incessantly to secure the establishment of general government hospitals in the state, to the end that those unfit for service might breathe their native air and be within reach of their friends. This persistency won the day and in Oct., 1863, a general hospital was established at Madison, the Gov. Farwell residence overlooking Lake Monona being selected. It was called the "Harvey United States Army General Hospital." Others were subsequently established at Milwaukee and Prairie du Chien. During 1863 the regiments on the

Potomac, in Missouri and Arkansas, and at Vicksburg were visited. The amount expended during the year was $13,999.91. A further sum of $10,000 was appropriated in 1864, which Gov. Lewis, used, as had his predecessors, with excellent results. The money thus spent saved many a life and encouraged the soldiers to greater efforts and sacrifices. Gov. Lewis visited camps and hospitals from Washington to New Orleans, up the Mississippi, and east and west, attending to the physical welfare of the soldiers; secured an order from the surgeon-general of the United States for the transfer of Wisconsin soldiers from hospitals south to those in their own state, and made it his special charge to see that they were sent home.

So closely allied is the sanitary department with the soldiers' relief work noted above, that it is well-nigh impossible to refer to it as a work by itself. In addition to the medical supplies, books, hospital stores, bedding, dressings, extra blankets, etc., were sent with each regiment and shoes and other articles were often furnished. After the large battles, supplies of bandages, sheets, shirts and sometimes dainties were forwarded. After the battle of Shiloh, 90 boxes of such supplies were forwarded within a day or two and divided as needed. The surplus of these supplies, after all who were ill had been cared for, was left with the sanitary commission at St. Louis. After Perryville a large amount of summer supplies were forwarded and used to excellent advantage, not only for Wisconsin soldiers but for others who needed assistance. Ample supplies and $500 worth of groceries were ordered to Murfreesboro. Supplies of vegetables were sent to the vicinity of Vicksburg in March, 1863, where much suffering existed. Later in the year another visit was paid to Vicksburg, also to Chattanooga and Chickamauga.

During 1864 large supplies were sent to Fredericksburg, mainly through the sanitary commission's Chicago headquarters, and 'to other points as rapidly as the needs and conditions permitted. Gov. Salomon appointed Hon. J. W. Beardsley as the state's sanitary agent at St. Louis; Mrs. Cordelia P. Harvey at St. Louis; Robert R. Corson at Philadelphia; Col. Frank E. Howe at New York; George W. Sturges at Keokuk; Godfrey Stamm agent in Kentucky and Tennessee; and George R. Stuntz agent in Tennessee. A Wisconsin's soldiers aid society had been established in Washington, and it acted as the agent of the state. The system of state sanitary agents was continued during the war, with changes in the personnel, acting in general with the United States sanitary commission, but with special reference to Wisconsin soldiers. Much was done, everything, indeed, which limited means would permit; but much more might have been accomplished, many little comforts given, had the state increased its appropriations by a few thousand dollars.

A history of Wisconsin's part in the war would not be complete or accurate without giving some space to the work of the wives, mothers and sisters during that time. The women of Wisconsin were early aroused to a realization of the part to be taken by them and were as quick to respond as were their sisters in other states. Almost from the first came a call for shirts, stockings and blankets, and without delay needles commenced to answer the call. Then lint and bandages were needed and delicacies for the sick asked for. Aid societies were formed in every community and when the United States sanitary commission was organized and branches established their assistance was invaluable. The Ladies Association for the Aid of Military Hospitals opened the way for organized, systematic efforts, and later the Wisconsin Soldiers' Aid Society was formed with over 300 branches or auxiliaries and united with similar societies of the north in the work for which all were organized.

Mrs. Cordelia P. Harvey, widow of Gov. Harvey, found her solace and comfort in working in the hospitals and on the field, giving nearly four years of her life to devoted efforts for the sick, alleviating their sufferings and bringing good cheer to those who grew weary with the long weeks of hospital life. Many of those whose condition rendered them unfit for further service, secured a discharge through her efforts and to the dying she brought peace through her own Christian character. She it was who made the application for a government hospital in Wisconsin, and although at first refused she persisted in her efforts, informing the president and the secretary of war of the real condition of the hospitals and the treatment of soldiers in many of them, how the hospitals were put in special order for inspection, and urging that the soldiers could be cared for much better in Wisconsin than in the southern hospitals. A telegram from Mr. Stanton Sept. 27, 1863, brought the glad news that he had ordered "the establishment of a hospital at the Farwell house in Madison, to be called the Harvey Hospital, in memory of your late lamented husband, the patriotic governor of Wisconsin, who lost his life while caring for the wounded soldiers of the state."

When peace came the work of the sanitary commission and aid societies was apparently ended. But as scores of straggling, footsore, sick and destitute men appeared, the need of further relief became apparent and the women of Milwaukee secured rooms in a block in that city for a temporary home, where the hungry were fed, the weary refreshed, the wounded cared for and the penniless furnished with means to reach home. Contributions and supplies were sent from all over the state. The legislature appropriated $3,000 and private contributions up to April 15, 1865, were over $6,000. The report of 1865 showed that up to that time 17,456 meals had been served; 2,842 enlisted men entertained and aided at the home; 2,000 more fed in camps and depots; nearly 400 received medical or surgical treatment, and many more were carefully nursed. Afterwards many thousands were entertained at the home.

The institution was incorporated and a state fair held in Milwaukee, through which $101,000 was realized, forming the nucleus for the beautiful national home which is now so prominent a feature of Wisconsin's first city.

A Bureau of Employment for Discharged Soldiers was also established in Milwaukee at the Y. M. C. A. rooms, and many a homeless wanderer was put in the way of securing honorable employment.

Writing of the work of the sanitary commission, the surgeon-general said: "In several of its important departments, be it remembered, this grand work is conducted mostly by the women of our country. When was there ever before a field of such unselfish, patriotic, useful labor, opened for the occupancy of woman, and when was ever an opportunity more gloriously embraced? Work on, ye women of America! In the history of this gigantic struggle, your deeds will add luster to the achieve-ments of our arms and go down in the memory of mankind 'to the last syllable of recorded time.' "

From the first the patriotic husband and father had been as-sured that his helpless ones should be tenderly cared for. When, at the close of the war, it was found that there were 8,000 orphaned children, the plan of a home for these little ones, which had been considered by a few led by Mrs. Harvey, met with ready cooperation. The owners of the Harvey hospital property offered it for $10,000 for the purposes of an orphans' home. Mrs. Harvey went to Washington and succeeded in securing a donation of the improvements made by the government, in the shape of extensive wings, originally costing $15,000. Residents of Madison and vicinity contributed $5,000. Repairs were made and by Jan. 1, 1866, it was ready for occupancy. In March the legislature passed the necessary legislation for its official organization, appropriated $10,000 for its purchase and an additional $25,000 for its support. Many children were cared for at this home, but the years brought all entitled to admittance within its walls to man's estate and its beautiful site on Lake Monona is occupied by modern homes.

During Gov. Salomon's administration he was requested to cooperate with other states, led by Pennsylvania, in the purchase of ground for a cemetery for the burial of Union soldiers at Gettysburg, and signified his willingness to do so. An appropriation of $3,523 was made by the legislature in 1864 in aid of the project. Seventeen acres were purchased and $63,500 determined upon as a sum required to enclose the grounds, bury the dead, beautify the place, erect a suitable monument and mark the graves. The bodies of Wisconsin soldiers were removed to the designated plat and appropriate headboards furnished.

The total number of troops furnished to the ranks of the Union army by Wisconsin under all calls from the general government during the war was 91,379. The following is a classification of the terms of service in the several years of the rebellion: Volunteer enlistments in 1861, three years, 21,815; 1862, 18,479; 1863, 2,943; 1864, 8,285; veteran reenlistments in 1864, 5,782; volunteer reenlistments in 1865, 246; draft in 1863, three years, 5,961. Total, three years' service 63,511.

Volunteer enlistments in 1864, one year, 9,102; draft of 1864, one year, 1,918; volunteer enlistments in 1865, one year, 9,678; draft of 1865, one year, 2,465. Total, one year's service, 23,163.

Draft of 1862, nine months, 961; first three months regiment, 1861, 810; 100-day service, 1864, 2,134; naval and southern recruits, terms of service not given, 743. Grand total 91,379.

REGISTER OF REGIMENTS

First Infantry

Cols., John C. Starkweather, George B. Bingham; Lieut.-Cols., Charles L. Harris, David H. Lane, George B. Bingham, Henry A. Mitchell; Majs., David H. Lane, George B. Bingham, Henry A. Mitchell, Donald C. McVean, Thomas H. Green. This regiment was organized as a 90-day regiment under the proclamation of April 16, 1861, with a numerical strength of 810, and left the state June 9. It led the advance on Martinsburg, participated in the battle of Falling Waters, and was mustered out Aug. 22, 1861. It was reorganized as a three year regiment and mustered in Oct. 19, with a strength of 945. Col. Starkweather was placed in command of the 28th brigade, Sept. 3, 1862, and Lieut.-Col. Bingham was advanced to colonel, Maj. Mitchell to lieutenant-colonel, and Capt. Donald C. McVean was appointed major. The regiment participated in the battles of Perryville, Stone's river, Chickamauga and Missionary ridge. It was mustered out Oct. 21, 1864. The original organization of 810 lost 91 by death, desertion, transfer and discharge, and mustered out, 719. The reorganization, numbering 945, was increased by recruiting, drafting and reenlistment of veterans to 1,508; losses, by death, 235; by desertion, 57; by transfer, 47; by discharge, 298; mustered out, 871.

Second Infantry

Cols., S. Park Coon, Edgar O'Conner, Lucius Fairchild, John Mansfield; Lieut.-Cols., Henry W. Peck, Duncan McDonald, Thomas S. Alien, George H. Stevens, William L. Parsons; Maj., George H. Otis. This regiment was organized in May, 1861, and was mustered in June 11, with a numerical strength of 1,051. It left the state on June 20 and was the first regiment of three years men to appear in Washington. It was brigaded with three New York regiments under command of Col. W. T. Sherman, Col. Coon being detached for staff duty. The regiment participated in the first battle of Bull Run, losing 30 killed, 125 wounded and 65 missing. It was transferred from Col. Sherman's command to that of Brig. Gen. Rufus King, commanding a brigade consisting of the 5th and 6th Wis. and 19th Ind. infantry. Co. K was detached permanently and organized as heavy artillery, a new Co. K being mustered. Later Gen. King was succeeded by Col.

Lysander Cutler and from Dec., 1861, the history of the regiment is merged with that of the famous "Iron Brigade" until it was detached in May, 1864, its loss being the greatest in proportion to numbers of any regiment engaged in the Civil war. The "Iron Brigade" consisted of the 2nd, 6th and 7th Wis., 19th Ind. and 24th Mich. At Bull Run the 2nd regiment bore the brunt of a determined onset by "Stonewall" Jackson's entire division on the Warrenton pike until the brigade could be moved into position and the enemy repulsed. The brigade held the line of battle until the army had passed on the road to Centerville, and was in a later engagement on the Warrenton and Sudley roads. It stormed the enemy's position as South mountain, the 2nd leading on the left of the road and the 6th and 7th on the right, routing the enemy. At Antietam the brigade dislodged the enemy after a severe conflict. At Fredericksburg it held an exposed position, subject to heavy artillery fire. At Gettysburg the regiment led the marching column and was the first to meet the enemy, (Heth's division), advancing upon it and receiving a volley that cut down over 30 per cent of the rank and file. Dashing upon the enemy's center, the 2nd held it in check until the brigade came into line, when the enemy was routed. At Chancellorsville, the Wilderness, Gaines' mill, Cold Harbor, Petersburg, and in numerous skirmishes, the "Iron Brigade" added new luster to the Union army, the 2nd Wis. bearing well its part. The regiment became so reduced in numbers that it was permanently detached from the brigade May 11, 1864, and employed as provost guard of the 4th division, 5th army corps until June 11, when it was sent home, the last company being mustered out July 2,1864. The members who joined subsequent to its original organization were organized into an independent battalion of two companies June 11, 1864, under command of Capt. Dennis B. Dailey. The battalion was assigned to provost duty; took part in the advance and assault on Petersburg and the skirmishes at Yellow house; was transferred to the 1st brigade, 3d division for guard and picket duty; fought at Hatcher's run; and on Nov. 30 was transferred as Cos. G and H to the 6th Wis., with which it remained until mustered out. To its original number was added by recruiting, drafting and reenlistment 215, making a total of 1,266. The death loss was 261; missing, 6; desertions,

51; transferred, 134; discharged, 466; leaving 348 to be mustered out.

THIRD INFANTRY

Cols., Charles S. Hamilton, Thomas H. Ruger, William Hawley; Lieut.-Cols., Thomas H. Ruger, Bertine Pinkney, Louis H. D. Crane, William Hawley, John W. Scott, Martin Flood, George W. Stevenson; Majs., Edwin L. Hubbard, Bertine Pinkney, Louis H. D. Crane, John W. Scott, William Hawley, Warham Parks. This regiment was organized in June, 1861, with a numerical strength of 979. It was mustered in June 29 and left the state July 12. It surrounded Frederick, Md., and arrested the "bogus" legislature; drove a superior force from Bolivar; was detailed as provost guard at Frederick in December; was attached to the 2nd brigade of Gen. Banks' army corps in Feb., 1862; took part in the advance on Manassas; acted as rear-guard in the retreat at Winchester; took part in the battle of Winchester the following day; fought at Cedar mountain, eliciting high praise; was at Antietam, where of 335 men engaged 27 were killed and 171 wounded; over one-half of it was at Chancellorsville where it lost heavily; it took a prominent part at Brandy Station; was at Gettysburg; aided in the preservation of order in New York city during the draft riots; did guard duty in Tennessee; took part in the engagements at Resaca, Marietta, Pine knob, Kennesaw mountain, Peachtree creek; accompanied the victorious army in its march to the sea and to Richmond; participated in the grand review at Washington, and was mustered out at Louisville, Ky., July 18, 1865. The total enrollment of the regiment was 2,156; loss by death, 247; missing, 5; desertion, 51; transfer, 98; discharged, 945; mustered out, 810.

FOURTH INFANTRY

Cols., Halbert E. Paine, Sidney A. Bean, Frederick A. Boardman, Joseph Bailey, Webster P. Moore, Nelson F. Craigue; Lieut.-Cols., Sidney A. Bean, Frederick A. Boardman, Joseph Bailey, Webster P. Moore, Nelson F. Craigue, George W. Durgin, Horatio B. Baker; Majs., Frederick A. Boardman, Joseph Bailey, Webster P. Moore,.

Nelson F. Craigue, Guy C. Pierce, Edward A. Ramsey, Erastus J. Peck, James Keefe, Henry Brooks, George W. Durgin, Horatio B. Baker, James B. Farnsworth. This regiment was organized at Racine in June, 1861, with a numerical strength of 1,047. It was mustered in July 2, and was first used in suppressing bank riots in Milwaukee and Watertown. It left the state July 15 and on the refusal of the railroad company to transfer it from Corning, N. Y., to Elmira, it seized the train and ran it to Elmira. It went into headquarters at the Relay house, Md., and later joined the "Eastern Shore" expedition, going to Baltimore in December. On Feb. 19, 1862, it left for Fortress Monroe to join the New Orleans expedition, but was sent to Ship island, Miss., until April 16. On the 28th Cos. E and G were landed 10 milesfrom Forts Jackson and St. Philip, after rowing 5 miles and drawing 30 boats loaded with arms and ammunition a mile and a half, while wading in mud and water waist deep. The regiment, with the 31st Mass., was first landed in New Orleans and took forcible possession of the custom house. The 4th Wis. was occupied in scouting duty in detachments until July 26, when it was sent to Baton Rouge, Col. Paine taking command of the troops there with orders to burn the city with the exception of the state-library, paintings, statuary and charitable institutions. This order was afterwards revoked on Col. Paine's representation to Gen. Butler that the town "would be useful to our army for further military operations." The town was fortified thoroughly by the regiment, which was later ordered to Carrollton, near New Orleans, Co. G being detached for service with the heavy artillery, and 40 men were also transferred to the 2nd U. S. artillery. The winter and spring were devoted to picket duty and small expeditions through Mississippi. The regiment took a prominent part in the battle of Fort Bisland near Brashear City in April. It was then sent to Opelousas, where it met and defeated a large mounted force of the enemy. By order of Gen. Banks the regiment was mounted and thereafter served as cavalry. It was in numerous skirmishes until ordered to Port Hudson in May as part of the investing force. It took part in the first assault and reached the ditch surrounding the fortifications, having been temporarily dismounted. It was in the second assault on June 14, losing 140 of the 220 men engaged in the charge. It returned to Baton Rouge July 25, and passed the following year in picketing, foraging and preserving the peace in that section, occasionally capturing or dispersing small bands of cavalry and guerillas. On Nov. 27, 1864, it formed part of a cavalry force to keep the enemy near Mobile from advancing toward Gen. Sherman. The winter was passed at Baton Rouge and the regiment was sent to Mobile in April, 1865. After the surrender of the latter place, the 4th was sent on a 70-day expedition through Georgia, Alabama and Mississippi. In July it was ordered to Texas and remained there until May, 1866, to prevent smuggling, guard against the Indians and preserve the peace. It was mustered out May 28, 1866. Its original strength was 1,047. Gain by recruits, 982; substitutes, 16; reenlistments, 260; total, 2,305. Loss by death, 350; missing, 23; desertion, 74; trans-fer, 2; discharge, 474; mustered out, 754.

FIFTH INFANTRY

Cols., Amasa Cobb, Thomas S. Alien; Lieut.-Cols., Harvey W. Emery, Theodore B. Catlin, James M. Bull; Majs., Charles H. Larrabee, William F. Behrens, Horace M. Wheeler, Enoch Totten, Charles W. Kempf. This regiment was organized in June, 1861, with a numerical strength of 1,057. It was mustered in July 13 and left the state on the 24th, being assigned to Gen. King's brigade. In September it was made a part of Hancock's brigade, 2nd division, 6th corps, with which it took a conspicuous part in the battle of Williamsburg and the Peninsular campaign. It was in reserve at Crampton's gap, but fought at Antietam, where Col. Cobb commanded the brigade. At Fredericksburg it was in Pratt's brigade, Howe's division, 6th corps. It was on duty in New York in Oct., 1863, during the enforcement of the draft; was one of the two regiments to carry the main fort and redoubts at Rappahannock Station; took part in the battle of Chancellorsville, and was engaged at the Wilderness, Spottsylvania, Cold Harbor and Petersburg. It was then sent to assist in the defense of Washington and was mustered out Aug. 3, 1864. An independent battalion consisting of three companies, was formed July 13, 1864, by reenlisted veterans and recruits, under command of Capt. Chas. W. Kempf, and accompanied the 6th corps to the Shenandoah Valley, being in engagements at Snicker's gap, Charlestown and Cedar creek.

The regiment was reorganized by Col. Thomas S. Alien, was mustered in Oct. 1, 1864, and joined the three veteran companies at Winchester on the 26th. It participated in the three days' engagement as Hatcher's run, in the relief of Fort Stedman and in the final assault on Petersburg, and won warm encomiums for its work at Sailor's creek, where it advanced through a swamp, waist deep, in the face of a galling fire and compelled the enemy to surrender. The regiment was with the 6th corps in the pursuit of Gen. Lee which resulted in his surrender at Appomattox. It was mustered out at Madison, Wis., July 11, 1865. The total enrollment during service was 2,256. Losses by death 285, missing 4, deser-tion 105, transfer 33, discharged 405; mustered out 1,424.

Sixth Infantry

Cols., Lysander Cutler, Edward S. Bragg, John A. Kelliogg; Lieut.-Cols., Julius P. Atwood, Benjamin J. Sweet, Rufus R. Dawes, Thomas Kerr; Majs., John F. Hauser, Philip W. Plummer, Dennis B. Dailey. This regiment was organized at Camp Randall, Madison, in July, 1861, mustered into the U. S. service on the 16th and left the state for Washington on the 28th. It arrived at Washington on Aug. 7, was immediately assigned to King's brigade and went into camp on Meridian hill, where it remained until Sept. 3, when it marched, with the brigade, to Chain bridge and was employed in picket and guard duty at Camp Lyon until it was joined by the 2nd and 7th Wis. and the 19th Ind. The regiment remained in camp, engaged in various duties until March, 1862, when it took part in the advance on Manassas, encamping near Fairfax Court House. On Aug. 5 an expedi-tion was sent out to destroy the Virginia Central railroad and the regiment, with a small force of cavalry and artillery, was detached and marched to Frederick's hall Station, where they destroyed 2 miles of the track, the depot and other buildings, and rejoined the command at Spottsylvania Court House. The regiment went into line at the battle of Gainesville and fought until darkness put an end to the con-test, losing 14 killed or mortally wounded and 46 wounded. The following day the regiment was present on the battlefield of Bull Run, where it lost 9 killed and 93 wounded. It participated in the battle of South mountain, fighting during the day and occupying the field all night. In this engagement the regiment lost 15 in killed and mortally wounded and 67 were wounded. It was vigorously engaged at Antietam, the story of which is best told by the casualties, 38 being killed or died of wounds and 106 were wounded. The regiment was in the advance of a storming party at Fitzhugh's crossing, where it crossed the river in pontoon boats and charged upon the intrenchments of the enemy. For its gallantry in this desperate charge the regiment received special mention in a complimentary order from Gen. Wadsworth. The list of casualties in this daring exploit show that the regiment lost 4 killed and 12 wounded. During the early part of the first day's fighting at Gettysburg the regiment had been detached as a reserve, but later it participated in a charge under a terrible fire and captured a Confederate regiment. Reorganizing the shattered ranks, the 6th moved forward to the support of a battery in its front, which position it held until the enemy had pressed back the lines on the two flanks, when it fell back to the support of the brigade battery. During the day the regiment saved the 147th N. Y. volunteers from capture by charging down upon the enemy who was pursuing it and in conjunction with the 14th Brooklyn drove the Confederates from the field. The loss of the regiment at the battle of Gettysburg was 30 killed, 116 wounded and 22 missing. In November it took part in the operations at Mine Run, and the regiment was successful in preventing the breaking up of a train belonging to the 5th corps. In December, 227 of the regiment reenlisted as veterans. It was accordingly remustered into the service and in January the non-veterans were temporarily attached to other organizations and the regiment returned to Wisconsin on veteran furlough. The regiment participated in the battles of the Wilderness campaign in the spring of 1864. It lost from May 5 to June 10, 44 killed and 110 wounded, and from June 11 to July 1, 17 killed and 31 wounded, which was increased during the following month by 7 killed and a number wounded. The regiment fought with its accustomed gallantry at Dabney's mill, in Feb., 1865, and lost 18 killed and a larger number wounded. It took a prominent part in the famous battle of Five Forks and a few days later had the proud satisfaction of assisting in the capture of the army of Gen. Lee at Appomattox Court House. In the short campaign, from March 29 to April 9, the casualties in the regiment were 16 killed and a number wounded. It moved to Black and White's Station, where it remained in camp until ordered to Washington, arriving there in time to participate in the grand review, and thence was ordered to Louisville, where it was mustered out on July 14. The original strength of the regiment was 1,108; gain by recruits, reenlistments, drafted men and substitutes, 1,035; total, 2,143- Losses by death, 322; missing, 7; desertions, 79; transfer, 75; discharged, 513; mustered out, 1,147.

SEVENTH INFANTRY

Cols., Joseph Van Dor, William W. Robinson; Lieut.-Cols. Charles A. Hamilton, John B. Callis, Mark Finnicum, Hollon Richardson; Majs., George Bill, George S. Hoyt. This regiment, organized in Aug., 1861, was mustered into the U. S. service by companies and left the state for Washington on Sept. 21. It reached Washington on Sept. 26 and joined King's brigade at Camp Lyon on Oct. 2. It participated in all the movements of its brigade during the following winter and spring and had its first skirmish with the enemy in July, 1862. An expedition was sent out by Gen. King to destroy the Virginia Central railroad, of which expedition the regiment formed a part, and during the movement a skirmish occurred with the enemy's cavalry, but the troops suffered more from the excessive heat of the weather. The regiment took part in the celebrated retreat of Gen. Pope, taking position at Beverly ford after crossing the Rappahannock, and for 3 days skirmished with the enemy, losing 2 men wounded. But it had its first introduction to real warfare at Gainesville, where the fearful list of casualties proved the desperate nature of the contest. All the field officers of the regiment were wounded, and it lost 46 men killed or died of wounds. On the following day it was present at the battle field of Bull Run, where it was temporarily consolidated into six companies and took part in the contest. It acted as part of the rear-guard on the retreat and during these two days lost 5 killed and 135 wounded. The regiment was engaged throughout the battle of South mountain and held its ground until late in the night, when it was relieved. It lost during the day 20 killed and 105 wounded. At Antietam the regiment was hotly engaged and lost 17 killed and 25 wounded.   It took part in the battle of Fredericksburg, but owing to the position it held it did not become very actively engaged and it lost but 1 man killed. At the opening of the Chancellorsville campaign in the spring of 1863 the regiment was with the brigade when it crossed the river at Fitzhugh's crossing in pontoon boats and drove the enemy out at the point of the bayonet.   In this affair the regiment lost 4 killed and 5 wounded.   Early in June it took part in a cavalry reconnoissance towards Culpeper Court house and as infantry support in the battle of Brandy Station did very effective service.   It bore its share in the battle of Gettysburg with characteristic gallantry and suffered severely, its loss being 33 killed and 80 wounded.   It was in the affair at Buckland mills in October, where it had the misfortune to lose 30 men captured.   In December 211 of the 7th reenlisted as veterans.   This was sufficient to constitute a veteran regiment and in January the non-veterans were temporarily attached to other organizations, while the regiment returned to Wisconsin on veteran furlough.   During the first day's fighting in the Wilderness, the regiment suffered severely, but in the attack on the enemy's first line it captured the colors of the 48th Va.   The battle was resumed at daylight the following morning, when the regiment participated in the grand charge upon the Confederates in front and was the only regiment that succeeded in holding for a short time the enemy's first line of breastworks.   At Spottsylvania the enemy established a body of sharpshooters within 50 yards of the Federal breastworks, but they were driven out by a company of the 7th Wis.   On the following day the brigade again advanced to charge the enemy's works in front, the regiment being on the left.   The troops to the left of the brigade were repulsed, and the 7th was obliged to return to its breastworks, which it did in good order.   It was the first regiment to relieve Hancock's corps at the "bloody angle" and took position in the enemy's first line of intrenchments, which had been captured by Hancock earlier in the day.   The list of killed and those who died from wounds in this campaign from May 5 to June 10 show that the regiment lost 92, while 184 were wounded. On June 18 the regiment advanced with its brigade across an open field, about 2 miles from Petersburg, against the heavy works of the enemy, through a galling and terrific fire.   In this movement the regiment was left without any connecting line on its left, but the ground was held for an hour and a half, during which the regiment suffered terribly from the infantry and artillery fire of the enemy. The federal batteries were firing over the heads of the men in order to prevent the Confederates from advancing from their works and having to aim low many of the shells struck in close proximity to the regiment. Having a few shovels, earthworks on the left flank were commenced, the soldiers aiding the shovelers with their bayonets and tin plates. Before they could finish their works, however, the Confederates advanced to within 75 yards, and after fighting them as long as there was a chance of holding the position, the regiment was compelled to fall back, through a more deadly fire than that through which it had advanced, returning to near the position from which it had moved in the morning. The casualties in the regiment were 21 killed and 37 wounded. On July 30 the regiment took part in the operations connected with the explosion of the mine and had 1 man killed and 1 wounded. In the desperate fight on the Weldon railroad the 7th captured 26 prisoners without sustaining any loss. On Aug. 20 it rejoined the brigade on the west side of the railroad and assisted in the gallant repulse of the enemy on the 21st, the regiment capturing the battleflag and all the field officers of the 16th Miss. The regiment fought with its accustomed gallantry at the battle of Dabney's mill in Feb., 1865, with a loss of 4 killed and 19 wounded. It fought at Gravelly run in March, and took a prominent part in the famous battle of Five Forks, which immediately preceded the fall of Richmond. It then joined in the pursuit of the enemy and had the proud satisfaction of assisting in the capture of the army of Gen. Lee at Appomattox Court House. In this short campaign from March 29 to April 9 the casualties in the 7th regiment were 18 killed and 52 wounded. After the surrender of the Confederate forces the regiment moved to Black and White's Station, where it remained until ordered to Washington, where it participated in the grand review. On June 17 it was ordered to Louisville, where it was mustered out and started for Wisconsin on July 2. The original strength of the regiment was 1,029; gain by recruits in 1863, 74; in 1864, 343; in 1865, 12; by substitutes, 189; by draft, 67; by veteran reenlistments, 218; total, 1,932. Losses by death, 385; missing, 12; by desertion, 44; by transfer, 106; discharged, 473; mustered out, 912.

EIGHTH INFANTRY

Cols., Robert C. Murphy, George W. Robbins, John W. Jefferson, William B. Britton; Lieut.-Cols., George W. Robbins, John W. Jefferson, William B. Britton, James O. Bartlett, Duncan A. Kennedy. This regiment, known as the "Eagle Regiment" was organized Sept. 4, 1861, with a numerical strength of 973. It was mustered in Sept. 13 and left the state Oct. 12 for the lower Mississippi. It took part in the actions at Greenville, Island No. 10, Farmington, Corinth, Iuka, Henderson's hill, Pleasant Hill, Cloutierville, Bayou Lamourie, Atchafalaya river, Lake Chicot, Jackson, Haynes' bluff, Vicksburg, Richmond, La., and Nashville. The general commanding at Farmington, in general orders, said, "The Badger state may feel proud to have the honor of being represented by so gallant a regiment as the 8th Wisconsin." Gen. Sherman highly complimented the regiment for doing "its whole duty in the camp, on the march and in battle," for "Pecular courage and gallantry at Jackson and throughout the siege of Vicksburg," and for other services. The original strength of 973 was augmented to a total enrollment of 1,643. Losses by death 255, missing 3, desertion 60, transfer 41, discharge 320. It was mustered out at Demopolis, Ala., Sept. 5, 1865, with 964 men.

NINTH INFANTRY

Cols., Frederick Salomon, Arthur Jacobi; Lieut.-Cols., A. George Wriesberg, Henry Orff, Arthur Jacobi, Herman Schlueter, George Eckhardt. This was a German regiment and was organized in the fall of 1861, under general orders of Aug. 26. Its numerical strength was 870 and it was mustered in Oct. 26. It left the state Jan. 22, 1862, and first took part in the "Southwestern Expedition" into Kansas, Missouri and the Indian Territory. It routed two Confederate camps at Cowskin prairie, as well as a large camp of Confederate Indians en route, and took part in an engagement at Newtonia against a superior force pending the arrival of the main body. It fought at Cane Hill, Prairie

Grove, Terre Noir, Miss., Poison springs and Jenkins' ferry. It was mustered out Jan. 30, 1866. The foregoing does not do this regiment full justice. Its membership included a large number of veterans of the German army. It was a well disciplined body, organized with Gen. Fremont's promise that it should be joined to Gen. Sigel's command, and it expected to be sent to the front at once. Instead it was sent on arduous, disheartening campaigns among scattered bands of guerrillas and Indians, suffering great privations and being in small engagements. Through all, in the face of keen disappointment, it maintained the traditions of the army of the Fatherland, performed well its duty, and won praise for its gallantry. Its total enrollment was 1,422. Losses by death 175, desertion 25, transfer 7, discharge 191.

TENTH INFANTRY

Cols., Alfred R. Chapin, John G. McMynn, Duncan McKercher; Lieut.-Cols., Joshua J. Guppey, John G. McMynn, John H. Ely, Jacob W. Roby; Majs., John G. McMynn, Henry O. Johnson, John H. Ely, Duncan McKercher, Robert Harkness. This regiment was organized at Milwaukee and was mustered in Oct. 14, 1861, with a numerical strength of 916. It left the state Nov. 9, and the following spring made a march upon Bowling Green, dislodged the enemy at Huntsville, where it captured the military road, machine shops, engines and rolling stock, seized Stevenson, Decatur and Tuscumbia, and elicited high praise from Brig.-Gen. Mitchell. It defended and saved Paint Rock bridge, acted as rear-guard in the retrograde movement to the Ohio, in which it fought guerrillas at almost every step, brought trains safely from Huntsville to Stevenson, and assisted in repelling an attack at the latter place. It was under a heavy fire at Perryville, Ky., and at one time held its position with empty guns for 20 minutes until the battery which it had been ordered to support was placed in a safe position. Of 276 men engaged 36 were killed, no wounded and 1 missing. Gen. Rousseau said in his report: "For this gallant conduct, these brave men are entitled to the gratitude of their country, and I thank them here as I did on the field of battle." The regiment was engaged at Stone's river, remaining on the field for 4 days; was at Hoover's gap, and took part at Chattanooga under a terrible fire, losing 18 killed, 56 wounded and 132 missing, of whom the greater number were prisoners. It supported Loomis' battery at Missionary ridge, and in the Atlanta campaign participated in the battles at Dallas, Kennesaw mountain and Peachtree creek. On Oct. 16, 1864, the recruits and reenlisted veterans were transferred to the 21st regiment and the remainder were sent to Milwaukee where they were mustered out Oct. 25. The original strength of the regiment was 916. Gain by recruits, 105; veteran reenlistments, 13; total, 1,034. Losses by death, 219; desertion, 21; transfer, 23; discharge, 316; mustered out, 455.

ELEVENTH INFANTRY

Col., Charles L. Harris; Lieut.-Cols., Charles A. Wood, Luther H. Whittlesey; Majs., Arthur Platt, Jesse S. Miller, Otis Remick. This regiment was organized at Camp Randall, Madison, and was mustered in Oct. 18, 1862, with a numerical strength of 1,029. It left the state Nov. 20, and performed railroad guard duty until spring, when it was sent further south. It was in a skirmish with the enemy at Bayou Cache, Ark., and was then on duty along the river until the spring of 1863, when it was sent to take part in the siege of Vicksburg. The regiment took part in the battle of Port Gibson and received a special compliment from Col. Stone, brigade commander, for its splendid work. It was engaged at Champion's hill, and at the Big Black river, led the charge which carried the enemy's works, and captured several hundred prisoners. At Vicksburg its loss was heavy, the regiment occupying open ground which was swept by Confederate bullets. Several months were then spent in arduous though uneventful campaigning, but the regiment received Maj.-Gen. Dana's compliments in an order "for the perfection of instruction discovered in picket and guard lines." Over three-fourths of the 11th reenlisted as a veteran organization and after a brief visit home it was sent on an invasion of western Tennessee and northern Mississippi, engaging Forrest's cavalry en route. It was given outpost duty at Brashear City, Co. D being detached to Bayou Louis and Co. E to Tigerville. Continued skirmishes with Confederate cavalry, as well as scattered bodies of infantry, prevented the massing of Confederate troops, and the smuggling trade was broken up. At Fort Blakely, Ala., its last engagement, the regiment held the record of 4 years by conspicuous work, being among the first to plant its colors on the enemy's parapet in the face of a murderous fire. It was mustered out at Mobile Sept. 4, 1865. Its original strength was 1,029. Gain by recruits 364; substitutes, 62; drafts, 147; veteran reenlistments, 363; total 1,965. Losses by death, 348; desertion, 25; transfer, 9; dis-charge, 31; mustered out, 1,264.

TWELFTH INFANTRY

Cols., George E. Bryant, James K. Proudfit; Lieut.-Cols., DeWitt C. Poole, James K. Proudfit, William E. Strong; Majs., William E. Strong, John M. Price, Carlton B. Wheelock. This regiment, known as the "Marching Twelfth," was organized in Oct., 1861, at Camp Randall and left the state Jan. 11, 1862. The regiment was one of those selected for the New Mexico expedition, and did much hard marching for raw soldiers, but the expedition was abandoned. It was sent to Columbus, Ky., to repair railroads and rebuild bridges, and from there to Humboldt, Tenn., from which point it made numerous brilliant expeditions, clearing the country of guerrillas and bridge-burners. In the fall of 1862 it was sent south with the Army of the Mississippi, engaging in numerous skirmishes, notably at Hernando, Miss., and the Coldwater river. It was engaged in the investment of Vicksburg, with small loss; was at the second battle of Jackson, and at Big Shanty, where it charged 2 miles through the timber, capturing the first skirmish line of the enemy and dislodging a brigade from the rifle-pits, with only six companies. It was also engaged at Kennesaw mountain, at Bolton, Miss., in two fierce engagements before Atlanta, at Jonesboro and at Lovejoy's Station. Joining in the march to the sea, it assisted in the investment of Savannah and the Carolina campaign. It fought at Pocotaligo, tore up railroads, drove the enemy from Orangeburg, assisted in the capture of Columbia and Winnsboro, joined the triumphant march north through Petersburg, Richmond, Fredericksburg and Alexandria, participated in the grand review at Washington, and was mustered out at Louisville, July 16, 1865. Its original strength was 1,045. Gain by recruits, 420; substitutes, 177; draft, 25; veteran reenlistments, 519; total, 2,186. Losses by death, 294; desertion, 26; transfer, 64; discharge, 336; mustered out, 1,466.

THIRTEENTH INFANTRY

Cols., Maurice Maloney, William P. Lyon, Augustus H. Kummel; Lieut.-Cols., James F. Chapman, Thomas O. Bigney, Augustus H. Kummel, Charles S. Noyes; Majs., Thomas O. Bigney, Charles S. Noyes, Samuel C. Cobb. This regiment was organized at Camp Treadway, Janesville, and was mustered in Oct. 17, 1861. It left the state Jan. 18, 1862, for Leavenworth and moved from there to Fort Smith, Ark. to join the Southwestern expedition. Upon reaching Fort Scott it was ordered to Lawrence to join the New Mexico expedition, but this was abandoned and it was ordered back to Leavenworth. It was sent to Columbus, Ky., where it was placed on railroad guard duty, and later garrisoned Forts Henry and Donelson. It accompanied an expedition against Clarksville Tenn., where it routed the Confederates and captured a quantity of army stores. It was then employed in scouting and was engaged in a skirmish near Garretsburg, defeating the enemy. It drove Gen. Forrest's forces through western Tennessee, then marched to Stevenson, Ala., where it captured a supply depot and held it until reenforced. It assisted in the success-ful defense of Huntsville against Forrest and of Decatur against Hood. A detachment of the regiment dispersed the 4th Ala. cavalry at New Market. The regiment fought Hood in his attack on Nashville. Lieut. Wagoner and 35 men of Co. G were captured at Paint Rock river by a force of 400. After the fall of Richmond the regiment was ordered to Indianola, Tex., and afterwards to San Antonio, a march of 145 miles with the thermometer at 100 degrees and many broke down. Through all the seemingly aimless wanderings and hard marches, with few heavy engagements to compensate, the conduct of the men was admirable, and Adjt.-Gen. Gaylord says: "The tireless vigilance which relaxes not, day by day, and week after week, although lacking the excitement which accompanies the movement of armies, cannot fail to command our admiration and respect for the 13th Wis. volunteer infantry." It was mustered out Nov. 24, 1865. Its original strength was 970. Gain by recruits, 414; substitutes, 83; draft, 72; veteran reenlistments, 392; total, 1,931. Losses by death, 183; missing, 3; desertion, 71; trans-fer, 6; discharge, 321; mustered out, 797.

FOURTEENTH INFANTRY

Cols., David E. Wood, John Hancock, Lyman M. Ward; Lieut.-Cols Isaac E. Messmore, John Hancock, Lyman M. Ward, James W. Polleys, Eddy F. Ferris; Majs., John Hancock, Lyman M. Ward, James W. Polleys, Asa Worden, Eddy F. Ferris, William J. Henry. This regiment was organized in Nov., 1861, at Camp Wood, Fond du Lac, and was mustered in Jan. 30, 1862. It left the state on March 8 and went into barracks at St. Louis until ordered to Savannah, Tenn., on the 23d. It was in action at Shiloh, where it charged a Confederate battery and drove the enemy from the guns, but was compelled to fall back. It repeated this three times during the day, holding the guns the fourth time, and receiving the sobriquet of the "Wisconsin Regulars," for the determined bravery on this, its first field. It lost 14 killed, and 79 wounded and missing. It was made provost guard at Pittsburg landing during the siege of Corinth, and was ordered to reinforce Gen. Rosecrans in the advance on Price at Iuka. When within 2 miles of Iuka it was ordered back to Corinth which was threatened by the enemy and at the battle at that place it had the advance position in the line, the post of honor. In his official report, Col. Oliver, commanding the brigade, said of its work: "Col. Hancock and his regiment, the 14th Wis., there was no discount on; always steady, cool and vigorous. This regiment was the one to rely upon in any emergency. * * * They maintained their lines and delivered their fire with all the precision and coolness which could have been maintained upon drill." The regiment was at Champion's hill, the Big Black river, and took a conspicuous part at Vicksburg, losing 107 men in killed, wounded and missing, out of 256, in an assault upon the enemy's works. It remained in the front line until the surrender and was given the position of honor in the brigade in the march into the city. Gen. Ransom said: "Every officer and man in the 14th is a hero." It was the first regiment to enter Natchez. Two-thirds of the regiment reenlisted in Dec., 1863, and joined the "Red River", expedition, being in the engagements at Pleasant Hill, Cloutierville, Marksville and Yellow bayou. It was also in action at Tupelo; assisted in driving Price out of Missouri; helped to defeat Hood in Tennessee in December; assisted in dislodging the enemy at Corinth in Jan., 1865; and was a part of the force that reduced the forts at Mobile. Co. E and parts of other companies were detached in the spring of 1864 and attached to the 17th corps, being known as Worden's battalion, which joined Sherman in the Atlanta campaign. The regiment was mustered out at Mobile, Oct. 9, 1865. Its original strength was 970. Gain by recruits, 540; substitutes, 85; draft, 315; veteran reenlistments, 272; total, 2,182. Losses by death, 287; missing, 13; desertion, 97; transfer, 23; discharge, 407; mustered out, 1,355.

FIFTEENTH INFANTRY

Cols., Hans C. Heg, Ole C. Johnson; Lieut.-Cols., Kiler K. Jones, David McKee, Ole C. Johnson; Majs., Charles M. Reese, Ole C. Johnson, George Wilson. Lieut.-Col. Jones' commission was revoked, March 1, 1862, and David McKee was given the commission as his successor. This was a Scandinavian regiment and was organized at Camp Randall, Madison, in Dec., 1861, and Jan., 1862. It was mustered in Feb. 14, 1862, and left the state March 2, being ordered to Bird's point, Mo. Six companies were sent to take part in the siege of Island No. 10, and at the surrender the entire regiment was used in garrisoning and strengthening the fortifications. Cos. G and I were left as a permanent garrison and the remaining eight companies were sent to Kentucky and thence to Mississippi. They joined the Army of the Cumberland and were sent to Nashville; then returned to Kentucky and participated in the battle of Perryville, being exposed to a heavy fire, but not losing a man. The regiment was sent in pursuit of Morgan's guerrillas and returned with 50 prisoners and many horses and wagons, having destroyed guerrilla premises, a distillery, whisky and grain, for which it received Gen. Rosecrans' compliments. The regiment was in a sharp fight at Nolensville pike in December losing 75 killed and wounded, and on the 30th and 31st was in the advance towards Murfreesboro. This brought it into action at Stone's river, where it made a name for itself for endurance and courage, losing in two days 119 in killed, wounded and missing. In the battle of Chickamauga it was engaged in a terrific contest with the enemy's main line, being hurried into line on the double-quick to fill a gap, its accompanying regiment leaving it unsupported. An Illinois regiment was sent forward, but soon fell back, and believing the 15th to have done likewise, opened fire, bringing the 15th under fire from friends and foes and compelling it to break lines and escape as best it could. The next day it was ordered into a gap and twice repulsed the enemy, but being left without support and nearly surrounded, it was again compelled to break ranks and retire. It lost in the two days 101, leaving but 75 men on duty. At Missionary ridge the regiment was the first to occupy Orchard knob. It was in the advance at Buzzard Roost and Rocky Face ridge; in the engagement at Resaca, charging the first line of the enemy's intrenchments; was in the engagements about Dallas, losing 83 in killed, wounded and prisoners; in the assault on Kennesaw mountain; was in reserve at Peachtree creek, and was engaged in the battle of Jonesboro. The regiment then performed provost and guard duty until mustered out. Cos. A, B, C and E were mustered out in Dec., 1864, and the others in Jan. and Feb., 1865, at Chattanooga. The recruits and reenlisted veterans were transferred to the 24th Wis. infantry and later to the 13th. The original strength of the regiment was 801. Gain by recruits, 97; substitutes, 1; veteran reenlistments, 7; total, 906. Losses by death, 267; missing, 23; desertion, 46; transfer, 47; discharge, 204; mustered out, 320.

Sixteenth Infantry

Cols., Benjamin Alien, Cassius Fairchild; Lieut.-Cols., John Bracken, Cassius Fairchild, Thomas Reynolds; Majs., Cassius Fairchild, Thomas Reynolds, William F. Davis, John R. Wheeler, Joseph Craig. This regiment was organized at Camp Randall in Nov., 1861, was mustered in, Jan. 31, 1862, and left the state, March 13, for Pittsburg landing. It participated in the battle of Shiloh, where it was exposed to a heavy fire for the greater part of two days and sustained a loss of 245 men killed and wounded. It took part in the siege of Corinth from April 15 to May 29; also in the second battle of Corinth in October. It was engaged in railroad guard duty from the latter part of

Dec., 1862, to the latter part of Jan., 1863, and was stationed at Lake Providence, La., from Feb. 1, to the beginning of August, when it went into camp at Vicksburg until Sept. 28. It was then stationed at Redbone, Miss., guarding fords on the Big Black river and engaging in skirmishes with bands of Confederate cavalry until Feb. 5, 1864, when it again became a part of the garrison at Vicksburg. Its next important service was in the Atlanta campaign, and it was before Kennesaw mountain, occupying trenches and skirmishing during the most of June, 1864. In the battles before Atlanta in July, it sustained a loss of 123 men, killed and wounded. It was occupied in duty at Atlanta until Aug. 26, when it moved forward in pursuit of the enemy, engaged in skirmishes at Jonesboro and Lovejoy's Station, and went into camp at Atlanta on Sept. 8. It was on the march to the sea, took part in the siege of Savannah and in the Carolina campaign was engaged at Beaufort, Whippy swamp, and at Orangeburg, where it crossed the North Edisto, waded through swamps and drove the enemy from his position. It participated in the battle of Bentonville and took part in the grand review at Washington in May, 1865. Part of the regiment was mustered out on June 2, at Washington, and the remainder on July 16, at Louisville, Ky. Its original strength was 1,066. Gain by recruits, 629; substitutes, 88; draft, 174; veteran reenlistments, 243"; total, 2,200. Losses by death, 363; missing, 46; desertion, 115; transfer, 38; discharge, 386; mustered out, 1,252.

SEVENTEENTH INFANTRY

Cols., John L. Doran, Adam G. Malloy; Lieut.-Cols., Adam G. Malloy, Thomas McMahon, Donald D. Scott; Majs., Thomas McMahon, William H. Plunkett, Donald D. Scott, Patrick H. McCauley. This regiment, known as the "Irish Regiment," was organized at Camp Randall in the early part of 1862. It was ordered to St. Louis a few days after organization and on April 10 was sent to Pittsburg landing, Tenn., where it remained in camp until called upon to take part in the siege of Corinth. After the evacuation of that place by the enemy the regiment was stationed there for the summer and in October it participated in the second battle of Corinth. Its loss in this action was 41 in killed, wounded and missing. Gen. McArthur, the brigade

commander, complimented the regiment, saying, "Boys of the 17th, you have made the most glorious charge of the campaign." An entire brigade was routed by this one Irish regiment. It took part in the battle of Port Gibson and the next day pursued the enemy toward Vicksburg. It was in the battles of Champion's hill and the Big Black river, and in the siege of Vicksburg its gallant services received special mention. On June 8, 1864, the regiment arrived at Acworth, Ga., where it joined the army under Gen. Sherman, and was engaged in heavy skirmishing until the 19th. It participated in the battle of Kennesaw mountain, sustaining a heavy fire from the enemy's artillery for more than 3 hours, with a loss of 2 killed and 11 wounded. It took part in the battles about Atlanta in July, and later was in action at Jonesboro, and Lovejoy's Station. It was with Sherman in his march from Atlanta to the sea, and performed gallant service at Savannah, Columbia and Bentonville. After Johnston's surrender the regiment participated in the grand review at Washington. It was mustered out July 14 and soon after disbanded in Wisconsin. Its original strength was 941. It gained by recruits during its service 385; substitutes, 136; draft, 215; veteran reenlistments, 287; total, 1,964. Loss by death, 221; missing, 5; desertion, 157; transfer, 32; discharge, 448; mustered out, 1,101.
grand review

EIGHTEENTH INFANTRY

Cols., James S. Alban, Gabriel Bouck, Charles H. Jackson; Lieut.-Cols., Samuel W. Beall, Charles H. Jackson, James P. Millard; Majs., Josiah W. Crane, Charles H. Jackson, James P. Millard, Joseph W. Roberts. This regiment was organized in Oct., 1861. It was mustered in and left the state March 30, 1862, for Pittsburg landing and reached there April 5. The next morning, with absolutely no instruction in the manual of arms and but little drill, it was ordered to check the enemy's advance at Shiloh. It fought bravely, losing 24 killed, 82 wounded and 174 prisoners. "Many regiments may well covet the impressions which the 18th Wis. left of personal bravery, heroic daring and determined endurance," said Gov. Harvey. It took part in the siege of Corinth and then encamped at Corinth and Bolivar until Sept. 17, when it was ordered to Iuka to reinforce

Rosecrans, but was immediately returned to the defense of Corinth which was threatened. On Oct. 1 it met the advance of Price and Van Dorn and fell back to the protection of Smith's bridge the following day. On the 3d, the enemy appearing in force, the regiment burned the bridge, rejoined its brigade at the railroad, and retained its position until over-whelming numbers compelled it to fall back. It joined in pursuit of the enemy after the battle of Corinth, and on Nov. 2 proceeded to Grand Junction. In the movement southward it went to Holly Springs, then back to Grand Junction, thence to Moscow, Tenn., and Memphis, and from there by boat to Young's point, La., where it remained until Feb. 9, 1863. In the advance upon Vicksburg it took position in the battle of Champion's hill, and reached Vicksburg on May 20. It deployed as sharpshooters to cover the assault on the 22nd, and on June 4 went into the trenches where it remained until the surrender. It was then on guard duty until Sept. 11, when it was sent to Memphis, thence to Corinth and to Chattanooga, reaching the latter place Nov. 19. It joined in the attack on Missionary ridge and was on guard duty at Bridgeport, Ala., during the greater part of December. It went to Huntsville on Dec. 25, remained there until May 1, 1864; then went to Whitesburg for guard duty until June 19, and was in camp, garrison and guard duty in Georgia and Tennessee until September. In October it aided in the defense of Allatoona against repeated assaults of a superior force. A furlough was granted reenlisted veterans on Nov. 12, and the recruits and non-veterans were temporarily assigned to the 93d Ill., which accompanied Sherman's army to Savannah. The veterans were ordered to Nashville, reaching there Jan. 11, 1865, and were then sent to New Berne, N. C., where they encamped until the last of March, when they joined Sherman at Goldsboro and took part in the movement to Richmond. The regiment participated in the grand review at Washington and was mustered out at Louisville, Ky., July 18, 1865. Its original strength was 962. Gain by recruits, 226; draft, 271; veteran reenlistments, 178; total, 1,637. Losses by death, 220; missing 78; desertion, 208; transfer, 23; discharge, 265; mustered out, 843.

NINETEENTH INFANTRY

Cols., Horace T. Sanders, Samuel K. Vaughn; Lieut.-Cols., Charles Whipple, Rollin M. Strong, Samuel K. Vaughn; Majs., Alvin E. Bovay, Rollin M. Strong, Samuel K. Vaughn, Amos O. Rawley. This regiment was organized in the winter of 1861-62, at Camp Utley, Racine, and was ordered to Camp Randall on April 20 to guard Confederate prisoners sent from Fort Donelson. It was mustered in April 30, 1862, left the state June 2, and was on garrison duty at Norfolk, Va., until April 14, 1863. It was then on picket and guard duty at various points for about two weeks, when it was assigned to duty at West Point and Yorktown until the middle of August, and at Newport News until Oct. 8. It was then divided by companies for outpost and picket duty at points near New Berne, N. C., and was in several small engagements with the enemy. It was ordered to Yorktown, April 28, 1864, and on May 12 the right wing, acting as a skirmish line, covered the 3d brigade. It accompanied the general advance upon Fort Darling, carried the first line of the enemy's works, and occupied the road in the rear of Fort Jackson, where the next day the regiment was united. It was compelled to fall back by the furious assault of a heavy force, but it did so in good order. It took part in the operations about Petersburg, doing siege and picket duty in the trenches. In August the veterans were sent home on furlough but returned in October, and participated in the engagement at Fair Oaks, a force of less than 200 men being engaged and suffering a loss of 136 wounded and captured. They were joined by the non-veterans and the regiment was kept on picket duty in front of Richmond until April 3, 1865, when it entered the city and planted the regimental colors upon the city hall. It was on provost duty at Richmond, Fredericksburg and Warrenton until Aug. 4, and was mustered out at Richmond Aug. 9, 1865. Its original strength was 973. Gain by recruits, 187; substitutes, 54; veteran reenlistments, 270; total, 1,484. Loss by death, 136; desertion, 46; transfer, 152; discharge, 343; mustered out, 803.

Cols., Bertine Pinkney, Henry Bertram; Lieut. Cols., Henry Bertram, Henry A. Starr; Majs., Henry A. Starr, Augustus H. Pettibone, Almerin Gillett. This regiment was organized at Camp Randall in June and July, 1862, and was mustered in Aug. 23. It left the state on Aug. 30, going first to Benton barracks, St. Louis, then to Rolla, Springfield and Cassville, Mo., and Cross Hollow, Ark., the enemy falling back at its approach. On Nov. 4 the regiment started for Wilson's creek, joined Totten's command at Ozark on the 11th and reached Wilson's creek on the 22d. In December it made a forced march of 100 miles in three days to Fayetteville; was in the battle of Prairie Grove, where it charged the heights through underbrush and captured a battery of 6 guns. The cross-fire of five regiments of the enemy compelled the 20th to retire with a loss of 209 in killed, wounded and missing. Gen. Herron wrote Gov. Salomon: "I congratulate you and the state on the glorious conduct of the 20th Wis. infantry in the great battle of Prairie Grove." The regiment wintered in Missouri, moved to Vicksburg on June 3, 1863, and took position in the trenches, where it remained until the city's surrender. It then occupied Yazoo City as provost guard, was sent to Port Hudson July 21 and remained until Aug. 13, when it was ordered to Carrollton and Morganza. It was ambuscaded on the Simsport road to the Atchafalaya river, but lost only 1 man. It went to the Rio Grande on the steamer Thomas A. Scott, but encountered a violent storm and had some difficulty in landing. It was employed in fatigue, garrison and picket duty at Fort Brown, and was sent to Matamoras, Mex., Jan. 12, 1864, to protect the American consul and remove American goods. On July 28 it left for New Orleans, on Aug. 11 took position at Navy cove, and assisted in reducing Fort Morgan. On Dec. 14 it sailed for Pascagaula and started from there towards Mobile. It routed a body of the enemy at Franklin creek on the way, and was engaged in the vicinity of Mobile during the winter. On March 27th it went into action against Spanish Fort, being on duty and under fire several days and nights, and after the surrender of Mobile it remained in that section until June. It was then ordered to Galveston, Tex., and was mustered out July 14. Its original strength was 990. Gain by recruits,

138; substitute, 1; total, 1,129. Loss by death, 227; desertion, 41; transfer, 113; discharge, 222; mustered out, 524.

TWENTY-FIRST INFANTRY

Cols., Benjamin J. Sweet, Harrison C. Hobart, Michael H. Fitch; Majs., Frederick Schumacher, Michael H. Fitch, Charles H. Walker. This regiment was organized at Camp Bragg, Oshkosh, and was mustered in Sept. 5, 1862. It left the state Sept. 11, being sent to Covington, Ky., for the defense of Cincinnati. It participated in the battle of Perryville in the 28th brigade, and after a march of 12 miles on the day of the battle, was placed by mistake in an exposed position alone, subject to the fire of both friend and foe. It escaped utter destruction by breaking ranks, then rallied and took position in line of battle. It lost 179 in killed, wounded and missing, Maj. Schumacher being among the killed. It performed guard and provost duty at Mitchellville until Dec. 7, when it was ordered to Nashville. With its brigade it repulsed an attack on the supply wagons by 3,500 of Wheeler's cavalry at Jefferson, the burden of the attack falling on the 21st. Gen. Rousseau said: "This regiment, led by its efficient commander (Hobart), behaved like veterans." It went into the battle of Stone's river the following day, was sent to the extreme front, and for 3 days held position under a heavy fire. It encamped at Murfreesboro during the winter and spring, moved south with the Army of the Cumberland in June into Alabama and Georgia and arrived at Chickamauga in time to take part in the second day's fight. It "never faltered during the whole day, but often the second line would have to face about and drive away the rebels from the rear." On being ordered to retire it fell back "only to the second line of works, where, still fighting, surrounded by the enemy, Lieut.-Col. Hobart and about 70 officers and men were captured." The regiment was in reserve at Missionary ridge and then was stationed on the summit of Lookout mountain until the spring of 1864. It was in the advance on Resaca in May, 1864, and was the last to retire in the evening. At Dallas it remained for 6 days under fire, its skirmishers being within 50 paces of those of the enemy. The regiment followed Johnston in his retreat from Dallas to Kennesaw mountain, where it charged the enemy's skirmish line and gained position within 150 paces of the main line of Confederate works. It was in siege; fatigue and guard duty until the fall of Atlanta, took part in the battle of Jonesboro, and then went into camp at Atlanta. On Oct. 1 it was attached to the 1st brigade, 1st division, 14th army corps, and pursued Gen. Hood northward. It then rejoined Sherman's army, took part in the march to the sea, the siege of Savannah, the Carolina campaign and the march to Richmond. It participated in the grand review at Washington and was mustered out there on June 8, 1865. Its original strength was 1,002. Gain by recruits, 169; total, 1,171. Loss by death, 288; desertion, 40; trans-fer, 99; discharge, 261; mustered out, 483.

TWENTY-SECOND INFANTRY

Cols., William L. Utley, Edward Bloodgood; Lieut.-Col., Edward Bloodgood; Majs., Edward D. Murray, Charles W. Smith. This regiment was organized at Camp Utley, Racine, and was mustered in Sept. 2, 1862. It left the state Sept. 16 for Cincinnati to aid in defending the city against a threatened attack. On the 31st it was assigned to the 1st brigade, 1st division, Army of Kentucky, and for a time performed guard duty at Nicholasville. It was then sent to Danville, where it was occupied in scouring the country in pursuit of the enemy until Jan. 26, 1863, when it started for Franklin, Tenn. On March 4 part of the regiment under Col. Utley joined a large foraging expedition to Spring Hill and during the march participated in two lively skirmishes. On March 25 about 300 men of different regiments under Lieut.-Col. Bloodgood, while guarding the railroad at Brentwood, were surprised, captured and sent to Richmond, but were soon exchanged. The regiment then moved to Nashville, and in April to Lookout valley, near Chattanooga. It left Lookout valley on May 3, 1864, to take part in Sherman's Atlanta campaign. It had a conspicuous part in the battle of Resaca, this being the regiment's first real battle. Its loss was 11 killed and 64 wounded. It participated in the actions about Dallas and was engaged in three smart skirmishes during the siege of Kennesaw mountain. For its unflinching bravery in the battle of Peachtree creek, the regiment was highly praised by Gen. Hooker. It shared in the movements of the 20th corps during the siege of Atlanta and encamped in that city Sept. 2. It remained on garrison at Atlanta, occasionally engaging in foraging expeditions, until Jan. 2, 1865, when it joined the general movement north to Richmond, participating in the battles of Averasboro and Bentonville. It was in the grand review at Washington and was mustered out June 12, 1865. The original strength of the regiment was 1,009. Gain by recruits 143; substitutes, 130; draft, 223. Loss by death, 226; deser-tion, 46; transfer, 31; discharge, 196; mustered out, 1,006.

TWENTY-THIRD INFANTRY

Col., Joshua J. Guppey; Lieut.-Cols., Edmund Jussen, William F. Vilas, Edgar P. Hill; Majs., Edmund Jussen, Charles H. Williams, William F. Vilas, Edgar P. Hill, Joseph E. Green. This regiment was organized at Camp Randall, Madison, in Aug., 1862, and left the state Sept. 15 for Cincinnati, whence it was ordered south to join the army before Vicksburg. It was with Gen. Sherman in the assault on Chickasaw bluffs and assisted in the reduction of Arkansas Post. The action of the regiment was the occasion of congratulatory orders from division and brigade commanders. It then proceeded to Young's point, La., near Vicksburg, where three-fourths of the men were stricken with virulent diseases because of adverse sanitary conditions. The regiment was on scout and foraging work until April 30, 1863. It was brought into reserve at Port Gibson and entered the village the following day—the first Union troops to occupy it. It took the advance of the division at Champion's hill, doing such effective work as to call forth compliments from the general commanding. The following day it went into action at the Black River bridge, its brigade capturing the 60th Tenn. and carrying the enemy's works by assault. It reached Vicksburg on the 18th, and participated in the general assault on the 22nd, reaching the base of one of the forts under a heavy fire. It was on duty until the surrender, at which time losse's had reduced its numbers to 150 men who were fit for duty. It participated in the attack on Jackson, and was constantly on duty until the evacuation of that point. It then joined the expedition through Louisiana, going as far as Barre's landing near Opelousas, which it occupied the entire summer. The return march begun Nov. 1 and two days later a superior force attacked at Carrion Crow bayou, driving two regiments through the 23d's lines. Flanked on both sides, the regiment fell back, formed a new line when reinforced, drove the enemy back in turn and regained the lost ground, receiving for its gallantry the public thanks of the commanding general, though it lost 128 out of 220 engaged. It reached Brashear City, Dec. 13, and was ordered to Texas, where it remained until Feb., 22, 1864, when it returned to Louisiana. It was in the celebrated Red River expedition, was in the battle of Sabine cross-roads, and the action at Cloutierville. It was in camp at Baton Rouge from May 25 until July 8 and then proceeded to Algiers and Morganza where it remained until Aug. 18. It was transferred to the 3d brigade, 2nd division, 19th army corps, and was engaged in guard, post, garrison and reconnoissance duty until May 1, 1865. It was then ordered to Mobile, where it was engaged in siege, patrol and picket duty, and short expeditions until July 4th, when it was mustered out. Its original strength was 994. Gain by recruits, 123; total, 1,117. Loss by death, 289; missing, 1; desertion 6; transfer, 124; discharge, 281; mustered out, 416.

TWENTY-FOURTH INFANTRY

Cols., Charles H. Larrabee, Theodore S. West, Arthur McArthur, jr.; Lieut.-Cols., Herman L. Page, Edwin L. Buttrick, Elisha C. Hibbard, Theodore S. West, Arthur McArthur, Jr.; Majs., Elisha C. Hibbard, Carl Von Baumbach, Arthur McArthur, Jr., Alva Philbrook, William Kennedy. This regiment, known as the "Milwaukee Regiment," was organized at Camp Sigel, Milwaukee, and was mustered in at various dates from Aug. 15 to 21, 1862. It left the state Sept. 5, and reached Covington, Ky., on the 11th, whence it was sent to Louisville and assigned to the 37th brigade, 11th division. It was first in action at the battle of Perryville, and of its conduct the brigade commander said: "The 24th Wis. went forward with cheers and soon engaged the enemy's right, pouring in and keeping up a cross-fire which made sad havoc among them. This was the first brigade to break. * * * Both officers and men behaved with coolness and deliberation, marching to the front with the steadiness of veterans." The regiment proceeded to Crab Orchard and Bowling Green, reached Edgefield, near Nashville, on Nov. 8, and moved to Mill creek on the 22nd. It was engaged in the battle of Stone's river, losing 175 in killed, wounded and prisoners, after which it encamped at Murfreesboro until June. In July and August it marched to Cowan, Tenn., and Bridgeport, Ala.; participated in the battle of Chickamauga, sustaining a loss of 105 in killed, wounded and missing; took an important part in the storming of Missionary ridge, making the ascent under a heavy fire and carrying the enemy's position on the crest of the ridge; assisted in raising the siege of Knoxville, Tenn., and was then on guard duty until Jan. 15, 1864. On the following day it dislodged the enemy from a piece of woods near Dandridge, and was then assigned to duty at division headquarters until May, when it joined the Atlanta movement. On this campaign it was in action at Resaca and near Adairsville; was under fire at Dallas for 11 days; took part in the operations in front of Kennesaw mountain; fought at Peachtree creek, and was then on railroad, guard and garrison duty until Nov. 1. It was with Gen. Thomas through Tennessee and Alabama during the fall, fought valiantly at Franklin, one of the severest battles in which the regiment had been engaged, and Gen. Stanley said: "I will not absolutely say the 24th Wis. saved the battle of Franklin, but they had a great deal to do with saving it." It participated in the battle at Nashville in December and spent the remainder of the winter at Huntsville, Ala. It was mustered out at Nashville June 10, 1865. Its original strength was 1,003. Gain by recruits, 74; total, 1,077. Loss by death, 173; desertion, 71; transfer, 138; discharge, 289; mustered out, 406.

TWENTY-FIFTH INFANTRY

Col., Milton Montgomery; Lieut.-Cols., Samuel J. Nasmith, Jeremiah M. Rusk; Majs., Jeremiah M. Rusk, William H. Joslyn. This regiment was organized at Camp Salomon, La Crosse, and was mustered in Sept. 14, 1862. It left the state Sept. 19 for Minnesota to aid in restraining Indian outbreaks. This done it was ordered to Columbus, Ky., in Feb., 1863, and assigned to Montgomery's brigade.

It was sent to Snyder's bluff near Vicksburg in June, and assigned to the district of eastern Arkansas in the latter part of the summer and fall. The winter and spring were employed in expeditions into Mississippi and Alabama, the regiment having an engagement at Decatur, and then joining Sherman's army for the Atlanta campaign. It was in action at Resaca in the front line and under heavy fire, holding a hill against three determined charges and receiving the approbation of Gen. Wood. It was in the three days' skirmish at Dallas and at Kennesaw mountain was under fire for over two weeks. It was ordered to Decatur in July to guard a train, and part of the regiment, with part of an Ohio regiment, engaged in a hot contest with two divisions of Confederate cavalry, intent upon capturing the train. Though compelled to fall back to the reserves they fought to such effect that the enemy was held off. The regiment reached Atlanta July 26 and assisted its brigade in dislodging a force camped on a hill, after which it aided in fortifying it effectively. The regiment performed effective service during the siege; then accompanied the army to Savannah; proceeded north through the Carolinas; was in a spirited fight at the Salkehatchie river; supported the attacking forces at Goldsboro; participated in the grand review at Washington, and was mustered out June 7, 1865. Its original strength was 1,018. Gain by recruits, 312; substitutes, 6; draft, 108; total, 1,444. Loss by death, 422; desertion, 20; transfer, 65; discharge, 165; mustered out, 722.

TWENTY-SIXTH INFANTRY

Cols., William H. Jacobs, Frederick C. Winkler; Lieut.-Cols., Charles Lehman, Hans Boebel, Frederick C. Winkler, Francis Lackner; Majs., Philip Horwitz, Henry Baetz, Frederick C. Winkler, Francis Lackner, John W. Fuchs. This was a German regiment, organized at Camp Sigel, Milwaukee, mustered in, Sept. 17, 1862, and left the state on Oct. 6. It joined the 11th army corps at Fairfax Court House, Va., and was attached to the 2nd brigade, 3d division. It joined the movement toward the Rappahannock in December, went into camp at Stafford Court House, and then was on drill, guard and picket duty until April. It participated at Chancellorsville in May, 1863, being posted on a ridge in an open field with its right wholly uncovered, where it and the 119th N. Y., both under fire for the first time, were savagely attacked by superior numbers. The men fought like veterans until both flanks were doubled up and only fell back when destruction or capture was inevitable. The regiment lost 177 in killed, wounded, and prisoners in the two days' contest. It was engaged at Gettysburg under the temporary command of Gen. Schurz. Ewell's corps, far out-numbering Schurz's command, bore down upon it with terrible fury, forcing it back, although the men fought like demons for every inch, until a point was reached where the line could be reformed. On the second day the regiment became hotly engaged and was compelled to fall back, which it did in good order, contesting the way as on the previous day, and later acted as rear-guard in the retreat to Cemetery hill. Its losses during the battle were 210 killed, wounded, prisoners and missing. At Missionary ridge the regiment was in reserve the first day and in the front line against skirmishers on the second. In the beginning of the Atlanta campaign its brigade had the advance at Resaca; was engaged at Dallas; took position before Kennesaw mountain and had several sharp engagements in that vicinity. At Peachtree creek it was under a terrific enfilading fire from a body of the enemy concealed in a thick wood, and repelled at the same time an assault from the front. Col. Wood, commanding the brigade, said: "The brunt of the enemy's attack fell upon it; the brave, skillful and determined manner in which it met this attack * * * and drove back the enemy could not be excelled by the troops in this or any other army." The regiment was in the front line before Atlanta during the greater part of the siege and was in many skirmishes and reconnoissances. On the march to the sea it charged and carried the enemy's works 10 miles from Savannah, for which it received the compliments of its commanders. It was in the engagement at Averasboro, was in line of battle at Bentonville, supporting the 14th corps, and at the close of the campaign of the Carolinas marched to Richmond. It participated in the grand review at Washington. In an official communication, Gen. Coggswell, brigade commander, stated that it was "one of the finest military organizations in the service." It was mustered out at Washington June 13, 1865. Its original strength was 1,002; gain by recruits, 86; substitutes, 1; total, 1,089. Loss by death, 254; desertion, 31; transfer, 125; discharge, 232; mustered out, 447.

TWENTY-SEVENTH INFANTRY

Col., Conrad Krez; Lieut.-Cols., John J. Brown, Ten Eyck G. Olmsted; Majs., Ten Eyck G. Olmsted, Charles H. Cunningham. This regiment was organized at Camp Sigel, Milwaukee, in the fall of 1862, was mustered in March 7, 1863, and left the state March 16 for Columbus, Ky., for garrison duty. It made an expedition to Cape Girardeau to expel Confederate raiders and was sent to Snyder's bluff in June, for the siege of Vicksburg. It was attached to the 2nd brigade, 3d division, 16th corps, and remained at Snyder's bluff until after the capitulation of Vicksburg. It then moved to Helena and on Aug. 13 was sent to Little Rock, where it remained until March, 1864. It joined Gen. Steele's Camden expedition as part of the 3d brigade, 3d division, 7th corps; was in a skirmish near the little Missouri river on the march to Camden; took part in the action at Prairie d'Ane; fought at Jenkins' ferry; then returned to Little Rock until Oct. 3, when it was ordered to reinforce Gen. Clayton at Pine Bluff. It returned to Little Rock on the 22nd and was detailed for railroad guard duty, in which it was engaged until Feb., 1865, when it was ordered to New Orleans and assigned to the 3d brigade, 3d division, 13th army corps. It took position in the trenches before Spanish Fort March 27 and remained there until the evacuation, when it was then sent to McIntosh bluff. After the surrender of the enemy there it was sent to Mobile and from there to Brazos Santiago, Tex., on June 1. It was mustered out at Brownsville, Tex., Aug. 2, 1865. Its original strength was 865. Gain by recruits, 328; substitutes, 3; total, 1,196. Loss by death, 246; miss-ing, 4; desertion, 56; transfer, 57; discharge, 248; mustered out, 585.

TWENTY-EIGHTH INFANTRY

Cols., James M. Lewis, Edmund B. Gray;. Lieut.-Cols., Charles Whittaker, Edmund B. Gray, Calvert C. White; Majs., Edmund B. Gray, Calvert C. White, John A. Williams. This regiment was organized at Milwaukee and was mustered in Oct., 14, 1862. It left the state Dec. 20 for Columbus, Ky., from which point it was ordered out on several minor expeditions. It embarked for Helena, Ark., Jan. 5, 1863, and joined Gorman's expedition up the White river. It was detached and placed in charge of St. Charles, which place the enemy had deserted on Gorman's approach, the balance of the forces proceeding to Devall's Bluff. The regiment rejoined the expedition on the return march, was transferred to the 1st brigade and sent on the Yazoo Pass expedition. It was engaged in the operations against Fort Pemberton, and in minor expeditions the remainder of the spring. It was on fortification and garrison duty at Helena from May 17 to July 4, when the enemy, 18,000 strong, attacked the garrison, numbering but 4,000. The regiment did its share in the defeat of the enemy in that brilliant engagement. On Aug. 6 the 28th was transferred to the Army of Arkansas and marched to Little Rock, which place was reached Sept. 10. It was detached from the brigade Nov. 7 and sent to Pine Bluff for the winter. On March 27, 1864, six companies were sent with an expedition to destroy the pontoon bridge at Longview, on the Sabine river, but were left at Mount Elba to guard a bridge where they held a force of 1,500 in check and with the assistance of a small reinforcement repelled a charge. The regiment was on guard and defense duty at Pine Bluff until winter, when it returned to Little Rock. On Feb. 22, 1865, it was ordered to Mobile and was assigned to the 3d brigade, 3d division, 13th corps. It was in the trenches before Spanish Fort from March 27 until April 8; was then sent to McIntosh bluff; worked on fortifications until the middle of May, and was then ordered to Texas for guard and garrison duty at Clarksville. It was mustered out Aug. 3, 1865, at Brownsville. Its original strength was 961. Gain by recruits, 144; substitutes, 32; total, 1,137. Loss by death, 231; desertion, 31; transfer, 81; discharge, 221; mustered out.

TWENTY-NINTH INFANTRY

Cols., Charles R. Gill, William A. Greene, Bradford Hancock; Lieut.-Cols., Gerrit T. Thorne, William A. Greene, Bradford Hancock, Horace E. Connit; Majs., William A. Greene, Bradford Hancock,

Horace E. Connit, Gustavus Bryant. This regiment was organized at Camp Randall, Madison, was mustered in Sept. 27, 1862. and left the state Nov. 2. Upon reaching a point on the east bank of the Mississippi river, opposite Helena, Ark., part of the regiment joined an expedition into the interior, after which it was engaged in picket duty and expeditions until Dec. 23, when it moved to Friar's Point and established a camp. Four hundred of the regiment marched into the interior and put to flight part of Forrest's force. On Jan. 11, 1863, the regiment went to Devall's Bluff, Ark., where it captured artillery, arms, stores and prisoners. In February it took part in the Yazoo Pass expedition, returning March 1, when it was assigned to the 13th corps and sent toward Vicksburg, reaching Port Gibson in time to contribute greatly to the successful results of that battle. It was assailed by a heavy fire from the enemy on the top of a ridge, and from some woods on the right, but it held its position and prevented a flank movement by keeping up a terrific fire on the enemy. In his report Gen. McGinnis, brigade commander, made special mention of the regiment for its gallantry in this, its first battle, saying the men "fought like veterans." The regiment lost 71, killed and wounded. At Champion's hill, the regiment advanced with its brigade across an open field to a thickly timbered hill where the enemy was posted, opened a concentrated fire and carried the position by a bayonet charge, capturing some 300 prisoners. The regiment lost 114 killed and wounded. It joined the besiegers at Vicksburg and remained during the siege in the advanced works. It was engaged at the second battle of Jackson in July; was then on expedition, guard and picket duty during the summer and fall; was in the Texas expedition with Gen. Washburn's division, which saved the 4th division from annihilation at Carrion Crow bayou; and it was at Cavallo pass, where a strongly fortified position was deserted by the enemy, who blew up the fort and fled, opening the Texas coast from Matagorda bay to the Rio Grande. The regiment was in action at Cloutierville, and the battle of Sabine cross-roads. It returned to Algiers in July, 1864, was attached to the 1st brigade, provisional division, and was in a severe skirmish at Atchafalaya river. It was next attached to the 2nd brigade, 2nd division, 19th corps; was ordered to Clinton, La., thence to Morganza via Port Hudson; and on Sept. 3 was sent to St. Charles, Ark., where it remained on guard and expedition duty until Oct. 23. The remainder of the year was spent in heavy fatigue and picket duty and expeditions along the rivers. Early in Jan., 1865, it went to Kennersville, near New Orleans, where it remained until Feb. 5, when it joined the movement against Spanish Fort, and was in the trenches at that point until March 31. It was then ordered to Fort Blakely, and was present at its fall, and then served as provost guard at Mobile until May 26, when it was sent to Shreveport on the same duty. It was mustered out June 22, 1865. Its original strength was 961. Gain by recruits, 127; substitutes, 1; total, 1,089. Loss by death, 296; desertion, 39; transfer, 103; discharge, 184; mustered out, 467.

THIRTIETH INFANTRY

Col., Daniel J. Dill; Lieut.-Col., E. M. Bartlett; Maj., John Clowney. This regiment was organized at Camp Randall, Madison, and was mustered in Oct. 21, 1862. On May 2, 1863, Cos. D, F, I and K were ordered to the upper Missouri as guards for transports in the Indian expedition under Gen. Sully, from Sioux City, Ia., to Fort Pierre, Dakota. Cos. G and E were sent to Superior and Bayfield to keep close watch on the Chippewa Indians, who were stirred up by the Sioux outbreak in Minnesota. In August detached companies were used for maintaining order during the enrollment under the conscription act, furnishing guards for conscripts, recruits and deserters. The regiment spent the winter in the state. Detachments were ordered to various posts in northwestern Minnesota and Dakota in March, 1864, where they spent the spring and summer in campaigning under Gen. Sully against the Indians, guarding emigrants, making many difficult marches through wild country, and participating in a number of engagements. On Oct. 1, Cos. A, C, F and H under Col. Dill were stationed at Fort Rice, Dak.; Cos. B, E, G and K under Maj. Clowney at Fort Wadsworth; Co. D under Capt. Fulton at Fort Sully, and Co. I under Capt. Grier at Fort Union. The companies were reunited at Louisville, Ky., during the fall, with the exception of Co. I, which remained at Fort Union until the following summer. The regiment was attached to the 2nd brigade, 2nd division, Military District of Kentucky, and was used in prison guard duty, as provost guard at Louisville, and for garrison duty at Frankfort and Georgetown in detachments during the winter and spring. Col. Dill was appointed provost marshal-general of Kentucky, April 17, 1865. Co. I joined the regiment on June 22, and the organization was mustered out at Louisville Sept. 20, 1865. Its original strength was 906. Gain by recruits, 312; substitutes, 1; total, 1,219. Loss by death, 69; desertion, 52 ; trans-fer, 46; discharge, 340; mustered out, 710.

THIRTY-FIRST INFANTRY

Cols., Isaac E. Messmore, Francis H. West, George D. Rogers; Lieut.-Cols., Francis H. West, George D. Rogers; Majs., John Clowney, William J. Gibson, George D. Rogers, R. B. Stephenson, Farlin Q. Ball. This regiment was organized at Prairie du Chien in Aug., 1862, when six companies were recruited. It was ordered to Camp Utley, Racine, on Nov. 14, where the remaining companies were recruited, and the regiment was mustered in, Oct. 9. It left the state March 1, 1863, for Columbus, Ky., and was assigned to the 6th division, 16th corps. It remained there on picket, provost and reconnoissance duty during the spring and summer and was ordered to Murfreesboro in October. Cos. B, G and K were detached and stationed at Stone's river in guard and fortification work until April, 1864. The regiment was assigned to the 4th division, 20th corps, and divided into detachments for patrolling the Nashville & Chattanooga railroad, one detachment being mounted for dashes into the interior. The regiment was ordered to Nashville in June for provost guard duty, remaining there until July 3, when it was transferred to the 3d brigade, 1st division, 20th corps, joining the brigade on the 21st before Atlanta and remaining in the siege until Aug. 25. It took a position on the Chattahoochee river until the evacuation of Atlanta and was then on guard and forage duty until it joined the march to the sea. When within 10 miles of Savannah, accompanied by part of another regiment, it passed through a seemingly impassable swamp, charged the enemy in two redoubts commanding the road, and in the face of a severe fire carried the works. It accompanied the army in the campaign of the Carolinas, performing well its part in destroying railroads, building corduroy roads and foraging. At the battle of

Averasboro it was in the front line under heavy fire from noon until dark. At Bentonville it held an exposed position at the front and was attacked in front and on both flanks simultaneously. It was thrown back, but reformed behind a rail fence, where it was speedily reinforced and withstood five determined charges, inflicting terrible punishment upon the enemy. This closed its active service. It participated in the grand review at Washington. Cos. A, B, C, D, E and F, were mustered out at Louisville June 20, 1865, and the remaining companies on July 15. The original strength of the regiment was 878. It gained by recruits, 200; total, 1,078. Loss by death, 114; missing, 2; desertion, 52; transfer 33; discharge, 167; mustered out, 710.

THIRTY-SECOND INFANTRY

Cols., James H. Howe, Charles H. De Groat; Lieut.-Cols., William A. Bugh, Abel B. Smedley, Charles H. De Groat, Joseph H. Carlton; Majs., Abel B. Smedley, Charles H. De Groat, Joseph H. Carlton, William S. Burrows. This regiment was organized at Camp Bragg, Oshkosh, was mustered in Sept. 25, 1862, and left the state Oct. 30. It reached Memphis on Nov. 3, and joined Sherman's movement toward Vicksburg, but returned late in Jan., 1863, the surrender of Holly Springs defeating the object of the expedition. The regiment acted as provost guard at Memphis until November; then moved to LaGrange; reached Moscow Dec. 3, just in time to repulse the enemy's attack on Hatch's cavalry; was sent to Vicksburg in Jan., 1864, where it was attached to the 2nd brigade, 4th division, 16th corps, and took part in the Meridian expedition. It held a pontoon bridge at Jackson until the troops had passed and then destroyed it. The regiment was attacked in February by a brigade of Confederate cavalry, while destroying the Mobile & Ohio railroad, but it repulsed the attack handsomely. It returned to Vicksburg in March, thence to Memphis Tenn., Cairo, Ill., and Paducah, Ky.; up the Tennessee river, 200 miles, to Crump's landing; thence across Tennessee to Decatur, Ala., where it was attached to the 3d brigade, and was engaged in guard duty and building fortifications. Cos. A, C, D and F, with a small additional force, engaged in a sharp skirmish with a large body of the enemy in

May and was compelled to fall back. The following day the brigade, with artillery and cavalry, followed the enemy for 7 miles. The regiment, which was in the advance, met a portion of the enemy and drove them to their main force, where by an impetuous charge, the Federals completely routed them. The regiment also dispersed a small body near Courtland and then returned to camp. It was attacked by a superior force while guarding a wagon train at Courtland in July, but repulsed the enemy repeatedly, bringing the train safely into camp. The following day it was engaged in the action that forced the enemy from his works near Courtland. It then joined Sherman's army in the siege of Atlanta, was constantly under fire until Aug. 24, and it was in the battle of Jonesboro. It was transferred to the 3d brigade, 1st division, 17th corps, and was on picket and guard duty until October at East Point. It then moved to Atlanta and in November joined the march toward Savannah, destroying railroads and public property and skirmishing at the Little Ogeechee and Marlow. It remained in the vicinity of Savannah until Jan. 3, 1865, when the campaign of the Carolinas was commenced. It forced the enemy from his works at Rivers' bridge after an all day's struggle, losing 51 men. It repeated this at Binnaker's bridge and on March 3 drove the enemy back to his main line at Cheraw. It was in the heavy skirmish work at the Cape Fear river, and at Bentonville it advanced through a swamp, charged with the 1st division and captured the enemy's works. It was in the general movement to Richmond, participated in the grand review at Washington, and was mustered out at Crystal Springs June 12, 1865. Col. Tillson, brigade commander, said that since the war commenced he "had not seen a body of men that, in point of discipline and efficiency, excelled, and very few that equalled the 32d Wis." Its original strength was 993. Gain by recruits, 381; draft, 100; total, 1,474. Loss by death, 275; desertion, 58; transfer, 27; discharge, 189; mustered out, 925.

THIRTY-THIRD INFANTRY

Col., Jonathan B. Moore; Lieut.-Cols., Frederick S. Lovell, Horatio H. Virgin; Majs., Horatio H. Virgin, George R. Frank. This regiment was organized at Camp Utley, Racine, in Sept., 1862, was mustered in Oct. 18, and left the state Nov. 12. It was sent to Memphis and assigned to the 3d brigade of Gen. Lauman's division, in the right wing of the Army of the Tennessee, Col. Moore commanding the brigade. The regiment joined the movement toward Jackson and Vicksburg in November, building bridges enroute to replace those burned by the enemy in his retreat. It was transferred to the 1st brigade, 4th division, and went into winter quarters at Moscow, Tenn., suffering greatly for want of suitable food. It was transferred to the 16th corps, and on March 9, 1863, was ordered to Memphis. In April it was in the advance on the enemy at the Coldwater river, driving his skirmishers 25 miles one day and concluding with a sharp fight that night at Hernando. The following day the regiment had the advance and poured a destructive fire upon the Confederates, driving them across the river. It took possession of the fortifications at Snyder's bluff in May, then moved to Vicksburg and took a position close to the works, where it was under constant fire until the surrender. It attacked the rifle-pits on the night of June 4 with such vigor that the enemy was driven back to the main works. On the night of the 13th Co. D charged a hill, drove the enemy from the rifle-pits in confusion, but not being supported was compelled to retire, though it retook them the following night, when the position was held. On the night of the 21st six companies drove in the enemy's pickets and dug rifle-pits within 85 yards of a large fort. The ground was lost the next day, but five companies of the regiment regained it at night in a 15 minutes' fight and held it until the end of the siege. The regiment was ordered to Jackson and with the brigade drove in the enemy, capturing his ammunition train. The 33d made a reconnoissance towards the Pearl river, but met a heavy force and only escaped capture or annihilation through its steadiness and the coolness of its officers. It returned to Vicksburg and in August was ordered to Natchez., where it remained until December. It went into quarters at Milldale, until Feb. 3, 1864, when it joined the Meridian expedition. In March it was ordered to join the Red River expedition, reached Fort De Russy on the 15th, and was engaged in guard duty for the transport fleet up the Red river in April, but was compelled to return because of the Sabine cross-roads disaster. It repulsed three attacks of a large force at Pleasant Hill landing, reached Grand Ecore, and repelled an attack at

Cloutierville. It was in a severe engagement at Cane river the following day, defeating the enemy after a 2 hours' fight and was in reserve at Alexandria. It participated in the successful engagement at Moore's plantation; was in an engagement near Marksville; was in reserve at Yellow bayou, and was then sent to Vicksburg and Memphis. It left Memphis late in June on an expedition through Mississippi and repulsed two attacks on a supply train near Carmargo cross-roads in July. It held the extreme right of the front line in the battle of Tupelo and was in the charge that drove the enemy from the field. It was attacked at Old Town creek, but formed in line, advanced under a severe fire across a long bridge and causeway, and drove the enemy from his position with terrible punishment. The official report says of the 33d: "Too much praise cannot be awarded to officers and men for their gallantry, and it is stated with pride that during these actions not a man straggled from the regiment." It was engaged in guard duty and building fortifications at St. Charles, Ark., until Sept. 1, when it was ordered to Brownsville, and on the 17th set out in pursuit of Price. After severe marching under great difficulties, it reached Cape Girardeau, Mo., and proceeded to St. Louis, Jefferson City, Lamine bridge and Warrensburg. It was on guard duty at St. Louis, the greater part of November and was then ordered to Nashville, where it took part in the battle. It reached Clifton, Tenn., Jan. 2, 1865; was on train guard at Grand View, and rejoined the brigade at Eastport, Miss., on the 14th. It participated in skirmishes at Corinth and near Iuka, was sent to Vicksburg in February, thence to New Orleans, Dauphin island, Cedar point and Smith's mills, skirmishing at intervals. It arrived at Spanish Fort and was the first organized regiment to enter the main fort, having been under fire much of the time during the siege. It was in reserve at Fort Blakely, reached Montgomery, Ala., Apr. 23, Tuskegee on the 25th, and remained on provost duty until July 19. It rejoined the brigade at Montgomery and was ordered to Vicksburg, where it was mustered out Aug. 8. Its original strength was 892. Gain by recruits, 174; substitutes, 2; total, 1,066. Loss by death, 196; missing, 4; desertion, 22; transfer, 37; dis-charge, 170; mustered out, 637.

THIRTY-FOURTH INFANTRY

Col., Fritz Anneke; Lieut.-Col., Henry Orff; Maj., Geo. H. Walther. This regiment was organized at Camp Washburn, Milwaukee, was mustered in Dec. 31, 1862, and left the state Jan. 31, 1863. It arrived at Columbus, Ky., Feb. 2, where it performed camp and guard duties at Fort Halleck. On March 3 Co. E was ordered to Paducah, Ky., and on April 25 Cos. I and G were sent to Cairo. On Apr. 27 Co. A was detached and ordered to duty at Fort Quinby, three-quarters of a mile south of Fort Halleck, and on May 12, Cos. B, C, D, F, H and K were sent to Memphis. On June 1 Cos. I and G returned from Cairo to Columbus, on Aug. 14 the several detachments of the regiment united at Cairo, and on the 16th proceeded to Wisconsin. The regiment was mustered out at Milwaukee Sept. 8, 1863. Its original strength was 961. Loss by death, 20; desertion, 283; discharge, 186; mustered out 472.

THIRTY-FIFTH INFANTRY

Cols., Henry Orff, George H. Walther; Lieut.-Cols., Charles A. Smith, George H. Walther, Robert Strohman, Fred Von Baumbach. This regiment was organized at Camp Washburn, Milwaukee, in the fall of 1863, was mustered in Nov. 27, and left the state April 18, 1864, for Port Hudson, La., where it arrived May 7 and engaged in guard and picket duty until June 26, when it was ordered to Morganza and assigned to the 1st brigade, 3d division, 19th army corps, commanded by Brig.-Gen. A. L. Lee. The regiment was ordered to St. Charles, Ark., and was engaged there in scouting expeditions and guard duty until Aug. 7, when it returned to Morganza. On Oct. 1 the brigade set out on an expedition to Simsport, and during the expedition the regi-ment participated in several skirmishes. It returned to Morganza, proceeded thence to Devall's Bluff, Ark., landing there Oct. 18, and on Nov. 9 was sent to Brownsville, where it remained until Dec. 1, when it was again ordered to Devall's Bluff. On Dec. 14, the regiment was assigned to the 4th brigade, reserve corps, Military Division of West Mississippi, and was employed until

Feb. 7, 1865, when it embarked for the attack on Mobile. Landing at Mobile point on the 26th it was assigned to the 1st brigade, 3d division, 13th corps, with which it engaged in the siege and remained until the enemy evacuated the place in April. It was then sent to McIntosh bluff and there engaged in building fortifications until the close of the war east of the Mississippi river. In August it was assigned to the command known as the separate brigade, Army of the Rio Grande, and during the rest of its term of service was engaged in guard duty and upon government steamers. It was mustered out Mar. 5, 1866. Its original strength was 1,066. Gain by recruits 22. Loss by death, 256; desertion, 29; transfer, 11; discharge, 177.

THIRTY-SIXTH INFANTRY

Cols., Frank A. Haskell, John A. Savage, Jr., Harvey M. Brown, Clement E. Warner; Lieut.-Cols., John A. Savage, Jr., Harvey M. Brown, Clement E. Warner, William H. Hamilton; Majs., Harvey M. Brown, Clement E. Warner, William H. Hamilton, George A. Fisk. This regiment was organized at Camp Randall, Madison, and was mustered in in April, 1864. It left the state May 10 and was sent at once to Spottsylvania where it was assigned to the 1st brigade, 2nd division, 2nd corps, and was held in reserve during the engagement there. It supported a battery at the North Anna river and was in line of battle, but not engaged, on the following day. Cos. H and K charged and captured a line of the enemy's works on May 26. The regiment advanced toward Richmond, and took part in the battle of Totopotomy. Cos. B, E, F and G moved forward as skirmishers across an open field and charged a strong line of works, unsupported, in the face of a savage fire of grape and musketry from the front and an oblique fire from right and left, driving in the enemy's skirmishers and losing 140 in killed, wounded and prisoners out of 240 engaged. But it accomplished the desired end by forcing the enemy to concentrate on this point on the double-quick thus relieving the pressure at the left. At Cold Harbor the regiment led the advance across an open field under heavy fire and remained on the field all day, losing 73 men. During the siege of Petersburg, it was engaged in several severe skirmishes, including one on the Jerusalem plank road, within 20 rods of the enemy's line, when one-half of the brigade was captured by a flank movement, the 36th saving itself by a quick change of front. It was engaged in skirmishing, short expeditions and picket duty in and about Petersburg, including Malvern hill, New Market road and Reams' station where of the 186 officers and men engaged there was a loss of 138 in killed, wounded and captured. At Hatcher's run, when separated from its division by a heavy force, the regiment faced to the rear, made a bayonet charge, doubled the enemy's line, captured a stand of colors and more prisoners than it had men engaged. This brought forth warm words of commendation from Brig.-Gen. Egan, who wrote: "It was a short fight; that rebel brigade was instantaneously crumbled and destroyed, being mostly captured with arms, colors and officers, to a total number three times greater than the 36th *   *   *   I now depend upon them with my veterans." The regiment repulsed a charge at the same point in Feb., 1865. With other forces it charged the enemy's line at Hatcher's run in April, 1865, taking the works at an important point, which resulted in the entire line giving way. It then pursued Lee's army and was present at the surrender at Appomattox. It participated in the grand review at Washington and was mustered out at Jeffersonville, Ind., July 12, 1865. Its original strength was 990. Gain by recruits, 24; total, 1,014. Loss by death, 29 6; desertion, 21 ;transfer, 38; discharge, 214; mustered out, 445.

THIRTY-SEVENTH INFANTRY

Col., Samuel Harriman; Lieut.-Cols., Anson O. Doolittle, John Green; Majs., William J. Kershaw, Robert C. Eden. This regiment was organized at Camp Randall, Madison, in the spring of 1864. The first six companies were mustered into service the latter part of March and left the state for Virginia April 28 to join the army of the Potomac. On May 17, Cos. H and L joined the first six and the regiment distinguished itself in the first assaults on Petersburg, when it lost 7 officers and 147 enlisted men, killed and wounded. On July 30 it participated in the assault following the explosion of the mine, sustaining a loss of 7 officers and 148 men, killed and wounded.

It was at the battle of Reams' station, acting as the reserve in the unsuccessful advance on the South Side railroad, and when the brigade was compelled to retreat the regiment poured so heavy a fire into the charging enemy as to completely check him, then repulsed a second assault and with reinforcements held the position until night. The regiment was in action at Hatcher's run in October and the winter was spent in and about Petersburg, often under fire. In the final assault it supported the brigade picket line against Fort Mahone, which was carried, three companies of the regiment being the first to enter the works. It participated in the grand review at Washington and was mustered out at Tenallytown July 26, 1865. Its original strength was 708. Gain by recruits, 101; substitutes, 64; draft, 271; total, 1,144. Loss by death, 211; desertion, 29; transfer, 29; discharge, 195; mustered out, 680.

THIRTY-EIGHTH INFANTRY

Cols., James Bintliff, Colwert K. Pier; Lieut -Cols., Colwert K. Pier, Charles L. Ballard; Majs., Courtland P. Larkin, Robert N. Roberts, Charles L. Ballard, Frank A. Hayward. This regiment was organized at Camp Randall, Madison, in March, 1864, and was mustered in April 15. Cos. A, B, C and D left the state on May 3, being ordered to Arlington heights and from there to White House, Va., where they were assigned to the 4th provisional brigade, for guard duty. On June 9, they were transferred to the Army of the Potomac and assigned to the 3d brigade, 1st division, 9th corps, but on the 11th they were trans-ferred to the 1st brigade. They were under fire in the trenches at Cold Harbor, took position in the extreme front before Petersburg on June 16, and the following afternoon charged the enemy's outer line of intrenchments, capturing them at the bayonet's point. The same evening they accompanied the general advance, capturing and occupying a second line of the works. They then went back to the trenches, where Co. E joined them. Upon the explosion of the mine July 30, Cos. B and E took part in the advance upon the enemy's works, capturing a position and holding it until the afternoon, when they returned to the trenches. The regiment continued in the siege and on picket duty until Aug. 19, when it moved to aid in the capture

76

of the Weldon railroad, repulsed an attack from three directions simultaneously and fortified its position. It returned to Petersburg and in October was under fire for 22 hours at Hatchers' run, after which it took position opposite the "Crater" in the front line, remaining there until spring. It led the right wing of the victorious assaulting column at Fort Mahone on April 1, its loss being over half that of the entire brigade, and entered Petersburg on the 3d. It was in the grand review at Washington. The one year men were mustered out at Tenally-town June 2, and the remainder on July 26. The original strength of the regiment was 913. Gain by recruits, 112. It lost by death, 108; desertion, 55; transfer, 21; discharge, 208; mustered out, 640.

THIRTY-NINTH INFANTRY

Col., Edwin L. Buttrick; Lieut.-Col., Jacob S. Crane; Majs., Martin Throup, George C. Ginty. This regiment was organized at Camp Washburn, Milwaukee, in May and June, 1864, was mustered in for 100 days' service, and left the state June 13. It reached Memphis on the 17th, and was assigned to the 3d brigade, Col. Buttrick commanding. Co. A was detached for train guard duty. The regiment had a brush with Forrest's cavalry near the Hernando road, the enemy 5,000 strong, breaking through the picket line and entering Memphis. The 39th was engaged in detachments, in guard and picket duty until its term of service expired and was mustered out at Milwaukee Sept. 22, 1864. Its original strength was 780. Loss by death, 5; mustered out 775.

FORTIETH INFANTRY

Col., W. Augustus Ray; Lieut.-Col., Samuel Fallows; Maj., James M. Bingham. This regiment was organized at Camp Randall, Madison, in May and June, 1864, for 100 days' service. It left the state June 14, reached Memphis on the 19th, was attached to the 2nd brigade, District of Memphis, and was assigned to train guard duty and in the defense of the city. It supported a battery, which was engaged with the enemy during Forrest's raid in August, having marched at the double-quick nearly 3 miles, and after the skirmish it pursued the enemy 2 miles. It was mustered out at Madison, Sept. 16, 1864. Its original strength was 776. Loss by death, 13; mustered out, 763.

FORTY-FIRST INFANTRY

Lieut.-Col., George B. Goodwin; Majs., D. Gray Purman, Jesse D. Wheelock. This regiment was organized in Milwaukee in May and June, 1864, being the third and last of the 100-day regiments sent from the state. It had no colonel, its numbers being insufficient. It left the state on June 15 for Memphis, where it participated in the fight with Forrest's cavalry, being posted with the 39th in the rear of the 40th. In common with those regiments it suffered much from disease. It was mustered out at Camp Washburn in September. Its original strength was 578. Loss by death, 6; desertion, 2 ; mustered out, 570.

FORTY-SECOND INFANTRY

Col., Ezra T. Sprague; Lieut.-Col., W. Wallace Botkins; Maj., John W. Blake. This regiment was organized at Camp Randall, Madison, in Aug., 1864, was mustered in Sept. 7, and left the state about Sept. 20. It went to Cairo, Col. Sprague being placed in command of that post, and Lieut.-Col. Botkin took command of the regiment. On Oct. 15, Cos. A, F, D, I and C were sent to Columbus, Ky., to assist in the defense against guerrillas. Capt. George M. Humphrey of Co. C, was appointed chief of ordnance of that post and assistant inspector-general in charge of Fort Defiance. On Oct. 25, Cos. B, G, K, E and H were ordered to Springfield, where Co. B was assigned to provost duty and Co. G was sent to Marshall. Cos. H and K were afterwards sent in search of deserters and to forward drafted men to the rendezvous. The regiment was reunited at Cairo in the early winter, performed provost and guard duty until June, 1865, and was mustered out at Madison on June 20. Its original strength was 877. Gain by recruits, 130; substitute, 1; total, 1,008. Loss by death, 57; desertion, 18; transfer, 149; discharge, 138; mustered out, 646.

FORTY-THIRD INFANTRY

Col., Amasa Cobb; Lieut.-Col., Byron Paine; Maj., Samuel B. Brightman. This regiment was organized at Milwaukee in the summer of 1864. The first company was mustered in Aug. 8, the last on Oct. 8, and the regiment left the state Oct. 9. It was sent to Nashville, Tenn., thence to Johnsonville for guard and garrison duty. Col. Cobb, member of Congress from the 5th district, was appointed commander of the post, and Lieut.-Col. Paine, who was chief justice of the supreme court, succeeded to the command of the regiment. The enemy opened fire on the place and gunboats early in November, but it being wholly an artillery engagement the 43d was compelled to lie in the trenches without action. It left Johnsonville Nov. 30, encamped at Decherd on the Chattanooga road, and remained in that vicinity until the close of the war, engaged in guarding the railroad and dispersing guerrillas. It was mustered out June 24, 1865. Its original strength was 867. Gain by recruits, 38; substitutes, 8; total, 913. Loss by death, 70; desertion, 40; transfer, 1; discharge, 39; mustered out, 763.

FORTY-FOURTH INFANTRY

Col., George G. Symes; Lieut.-Col., Oliver C. Bissell; Maj., William Warner. This regiment was organized at Camp Randall, Madison, in the fall of 1864. Co. A left the state Oct. 10, and was followed by Cos. B, F, D and C, successively, the last reaching Nashville, Tenn., Nov. 30. The other companies reached Nashville in Feb., 1865, and the regiment was employed in post and guard duty until March 9, when it was ordered to Eastport, Miss., to escort the Union prisoners to be turned over by Forrest, but not getting them it returned to Nashville and left on April 3 for Paducah, Ky., where it remained on picket duty until Aug. 28, when it was mustered out. Its original strength was 877. Gain by recruits, 235; substitutes, 2; total, 1,114. Loss by death, 57; desertion, 48; transfer, 121; discharge, 92; mustered out, 796.

FORTY-FIFTH INFANTRY

Col., Henry F. Belitz; Lieut.-Col., Gumal Hesse; Maj., Charles A. Menges. This regiment was organized during the fall and winter of 1864, was sent by companies to Nashville at various times during the early spring of 1865, and was stationed at Nashville until mustered out July 17, 1865. Its original strength was 859. Gain by recruits, 142; total, 1,001. Loss by death, 26; desertion, 8; transfer, 85; discharge, 80; mustered out, 802.

FORTY-SIXTH INFANTRY

Col., Frederick S. Lovell; Lieut.-Col., Abel B. Smedley; Maj., Charles H. Ford. This regiment was organized at Camp Randall, Madison, and was mustered in March 2, 1865. It left the state March 5 for Louisville, but was at once forwarded to Athens, Ala., where it acted as railroad guard. Col. Lovell was placed in com-mand of the post, Lieut.-Col. Smedley assuming command of the regiment, and it passed the summer at that point. It was mustered out at Nashville Sept. 27, 1865. Col. Lovell was brevetted brigadier-general. The original strength of the regiment was 914. Gain by recruits, 33; total, 947; Loss by death, 13; desertion, 8; transfer, 31; discharge, 41; mustered out, 854.

FORTY-SEVENTH INFANTRY

Col., George C. Ginty; Lieut.-Col., Robert H. Spencer; Maj., Kelsey M. Adams. This regiment was organized at Camp Randall in the winter of 1864 and left the state Feb. 27, 1865. It proceeded to Louisville, Ky., Nashville and Tullahoma, Tenn., where it was assigned to guard duty until the close of August, and was mustered out Sept. 4. Its original strength was 927. Gain by recruits, 58; total, 985. Loss by death, 34; desertion, 23; transfer, 29; discharge, 87; mustered out, 812.

FORTY-EIGHTH INFANTRY

Cols., Uri B. Pearsall, Henry Shears; Lieut.-Cols., Henry Shears, Cyrus M. Butt; John B. Vosburgh. This regiment was organized at Camp Washburn, Milwaukee, in Feb. and March, 1865. Eight companies left the state March 22 and reported at Benton barracks, St. Louis, Mo. where they were ordered to Paola, Kan. Co. C was ordered to Lawrence, Co. H to Olathe, F and G were retained at Paola, and A, B, D and E were sent to Fort Scott. Cos. I and K left Wisconsin March 28 and arrived at Fort Scott April 28. Col. Pearsall was placed in command at Fort Scott early in May, and Maj. Butt was placed in command of all the troops in Miami and Johnson counties, with head-quarters at Paola. The regiment was employed by detachments in getting out timber for fortifications, protecting the country from guerrillas, constructing bridges, erecting new buildings, etc. On July 19 Col. Pearsall was assigned to the command of all the troops in and west of Neosho Valley, Kan., with headquarters at Humboldt, Lieut.-Col. Shears succeeding to the command of Fort Scott. Capt. C. W. Felker succeeded to the command of the regiment, and on Aug. 10 the 48th was ordered to Lawrence. It left that place Sept. 6, for Fort Zarah, Kan., where Cos. E and G were stationed, and the remainder of the regiment moved to Fort Larned. On Oct. 1, the regiment was divided into detachments and sent to various posts for the purpose of guarding mail and government trains against the Indians. Cos. A, H, E and G were mustered out at Leavenworth Dec. 30, 1865, Cos. B, D, F and I, on Feb. 19, 1866, and Cos. C and K on March 24. The original strength of the regiment was 828. Gain by recruits, 4; total, 832. Loss by death, 9; desertion, 67; discharge, 36; mustered out, 720.

FORTY-NINTH INFANTRY

Col., Samuel Fallows; Lieut.-Col., Edward Coleman; Maj., D. K. Noyes. This regiment was organized at Camp Randall, Madison, and left the state March 8, 1865. It reached Benton barracks, St. Louis, two days later, and was ordered to Rolla, Mo., for guard and garrison duty. Co. K was placed at Fort Wyman, I at Fort Detty and B was sent 10 miles east of St. James. Co. A was stationed at Waynesville in June, D at Big and Little Piney. In July Co. H was sent to St. Louis for provost duty, and Cos. D and E to Benton barracks as permanent guard. Col. Fallows was placed in command of the post at Rolla in March, and later of the 3d sub-district of Missouri. Maj. Noyes was detailed on general court-martial at St. Louis, Lieut.-Col. Coleman taking command of the regiment and giving it a name for discipline which elicited high commendations from the department commander. The regiment was ordered to St. Louis Aug. 17, for prison guard duty, Col. Fallows being placed in command of the post there and of the first sub-district of Missouri. Cos. B, C, and D were mustered out Nov. 1, and the remainder on Nov. 8. Col. Fallows was brevetted brigadier-general, Lieut.-Col. Coleman became colonel, Maj. Noyes, lieutenant-colonel, and Capt. Cheney was brevetted major. The original strength of the regiment was 986. Gain by recruits, 16; total, 1,002. Loss by death, 48; desertion, 6; discharge, 173; mustered out, 775.

FIFTIETH INFANTRY

Col., John G. Clark; Lieut.-Col., Edwin E. Bryant; Maj., Hugh McDermott. This regiment was organized at Camp Randall and left the state by companies in the latter part of March and beginning of April, 1865. It was sent to Benton barracks, St. Louis; thence to Fort Leavenworth, Kan., and in October to Fort Rice, Dak., where it remained until the spring of 1866. Co. E was mustered out April 19 at Madison. The remainder of the regiment returned in June and was mustered out on June 14. Its original strength was 942. Gain by recruits, 16; total, 958. Loss by death, 28; desertion, 141; discharge, 127; mustered out, 562.

FIFTY FIRST INFANTRY

Col., Leonard Martin; Lieut.-Col., John B. Vliet; Maj., Alfred Taggart. The six original companies of this regiment were organized at Camp Washburn, Milwaukee, in Feb., March and April, 1865,. and were sent to Benton barracks, St. Louis. Co. B was placed on duty at St.

Louis, the remaining companies being ordered to Warrensburg, Mo. for railroad guard duty, and were joined there by Co. B, on June 21. Co. A was stationed at Crawford's run, the others at Pleasant Hill. In June the four companies of the 53d regiment were consolidated with the 51st. Cos. G, H, I and K, of the 51st, did not leave the state, but were discharged on May 6 under general orders for reduction of the army. The regiment was mustered out by companies on various dates during Aug., 1865. Its original strength was 841. Gain by recruits, 2; total, 843. Loss by death, 8; desertion, 87; discharge, 34; mustered out, 714.

Fifty-second Infantry

Lieut.-Col., Hiram J. Lewis. This regiment was organized in five companies during the spring of 1865 and left the state by companies in April. It was ordered to Holden, 248 miles from. St. Louis, where it guarded workmen on the Pacific railway and furnished scouting parties for protection against bushwhackers. On June 21, it was assigned to duty at St. Louis and was mustered out Aug. 2. Its original strength was 486. Gain by recruits, 25; total, 511. Loss by death, 6; desertion, 42; transfer, 16; discharge, 41; mustered out, 406.

Fifty-third Infantry

Lieut.-Col., Robert T. Pugh. The four copanies of this regiment were organized in the spring of 1865, when the government ordered all recruits not mustered in to be discharged. They were sent to St. Louis and thence to Leavenworth, where the battalion was transferred to the 51st on June 10, 1865. Co. A became Co. G of the 51st, B became Co. H; C became K, and D became I. They were mustered out with that regiment in Aug., 1865. The original strength of the four companies was 380. Gain by recruits, 9; total, 389. Loss by death, 8; desertion, 14; discharge, 47; mustered out, 315.

Company G, First U. S. Sharpshooters

Capt., Frank E. Marble; First Lieuts., Charles F. Shepard, Charles A. Stephens; Second Lieuts., Charles A. Stevens, Ezzan H. Benson, Perrin C. Judkins. Col. Berdan, of New York, having been authorized by the government to recruit a company of sharpshooters from each loyal state, Co. G was raised in Wis-consin in Sept., 1861. No applicant was accepted unless he could put ten consecutive shots within 5 inches from the center of the bull's eye at 200 yards, when firing at rest. The company was organized at Camp Randall, left the state Sept. 19, went into camp at Weehawken, N. Y., and was mustered in on the 23d. The 1st regiment U. S. sharpshooters was organized with ten companies and on March 21, 1862, was assigned to Gen. Fitz John Porter's division in the Army of the Potomac at Fortress Monroe. It was under fire at Big Bethel, Va., for the first time, and was next in a skirmish at Cockletown in April, while en route to York-town. It was in the rifle-pits before Yorktown until its evacuation, 5 picked men of Co. G being the first to enter the works. It was engaged in the action at Hanover Court House in May, and assisted in the repulse of the enemy. Co. G was one of two companies sent to Gen. Slocum's. division. It was engaged as skirmishers at Mechanicsville; took part at Gaines' mill; suffered severely at Charles City cross-roads from a flank fire caused by the retreat of a regiment in front, but it held its position; was in action at the battle of Malvern hill, and lost heavily during the spring and summer, in killed, wounded and sick. It was engaged in the skirmish near Manassas; was in the second battle at Bull Run; was present at Antietam, but not in action; was engaged in skirmishing and as guard at crossings in the march of the corps to Blackford's ford, on the Potomac; was at Sharpsburg, Md., until Oct. 30, when it joined the army at Warrenton ; was ordered to Falmouth in November and went into camp, remaining there until Dec. 11. It participated in the battle of Fredericksburg and was selected to cover the retreat of all the forces across the Rappahannock. It was in winter quarters at Falmouth until Apr. 28, 1863, when the forward movement was begun with the 3d army corps, to which the 3d brigade, consisting of the 1st and 2nd sharpshooters, was attached. Co. G was put forward as skirmishers in the battle of Chancellorsville and engaged in a hot fight with a body of the enemy, capturing 60 in one squad, and assisting in the capture of the 25th Ga. in a railroad cut. The company covered the movement of the troops in recrossing the river, maintaining one position for 17 hours without being relieved, even to obtain water.   On June 11 the sharpshooters were assigned to the 2nd brigade, 1st division, 3d corps, with which they were engaged at Gettysburg, Co. G being posted on the picket line, where it checked an advance of the enemy on July 2.   It also aided in repulsing a desperate charge and in the capture of a brigade on the 3d.   As skirmishers it took part in the battle of Wapping Heights, and also took part in the action at Auburn, where it charged across an open space and dislodged a party of dismounted cavalry, forming a strong skirmish line.   At Kelly's ford, the regiment formed a line of skirmishers, drove the enemy across the river, prevented his reinforcements from coming up, and captured the rifle-pits, together with 500 prisoners, Cos. G and B covering the advance. Co. G formed the extreme advance in the demonstration against the enemy's works at Mine run, and then was in camp until Jan. 11, 1864.   It was transferred to the 2nd brigade, 3d division, 2nd corps and was in camp near Brandy Station until May 3.   In the battle of the Wilderness it was on the skirmish line and held an exposed posi-tion during the entire engagement.   It was in the battle of Po river, and at Spottsylvania participated in the charge of the 2nd corps, which resulted in the capture of 4,000 prisoners, 20 cannon and the first line of works.   The regiment was engaged at the North Anna, where Co. G supported a battery the first day and covered the passage of the river by the troops, a detail of 40 men capturing and holding several buildings close to the enemy's line. At Totopotamy creek, it was in continuous action and at Cold Harbor was sent with others to the front to protect the troops engaged in constructing earthworks. It   took position before Petersburg on June 15 and was in the first assaults on the works.   It was in the battle on the Jerusalem plank road, was also engaged at Deep Bottom, and remained before Petersburg on picket duty the remainder of the summer. Co. G was mustered out Sept. 22, 1864, the reenlisted veterans and recruits being transferred to other companies. Its original strength was 105. Gain by recruits, 80; veter-ans, reenlisted, 9; total, 194. Loss by death,

34: missing 8; desertion, 4; transfer, 43; discharge, 58; mustered out, 47.

FIRST CAVALRY

Cols., Edward Daniels, Oscar H. LaGrange; Lieut.-Cols., Oscar H. LaGrange, Henry Pomeroy, William H. Torrey, Henry Harnden; Majs., Oscar H. LaGrange, Henry S. Eggleston, Thomas H. Mars, Nathan Paine, Stephen V. Shipman, Henry Pomeroy, Henry Harnden, Newton Jones, William H. Torrey, Levi Howland. This regiment was organized at Camp Fremont, Ripon, and Camp Harvey, Kenosha, in the summer and fall of 1861, 600 men having been enrolled at the former place up to the time of the change of location in November. It was mustered in March 8, 1862, and left the state on the 17th for Benton barracks, St. Louis, for equipment. On April 28 it moved to Cape Girardeau, thence to Bloomfield, where companies were detached to various points in Missouri and Arkansas for scout and train guard duty. The companies were in several engagements, frequently with superior forces, and were generally successful, though at Jonesboro in August a small detachment was compelled to surrender to greatly superior numbers. At L'Anguille ferry, Ark., occurred one of the fiercest engagements of the war, when Maj. Eggleston, with 130 men, was attacked by 500 Texas Rangers, the enemy overwhelming the little company and only about 20 escaping. The regiment with the exception of detachments moved towards Helena and reached its destination early in August. It was ordered back to Cape Girardeau in September after terrible hardships, wading through swamps, without adequate supplies, drinking foul water, burdened by sick members, and being finally reduced to nearly half its original strength. It was ordered to Greenville in early October and on the 19th to Patterson, where it was stationed during November and December, engaged in dispersing guerrillas, picking up small bodies of the enemy and foraging. On Dec. 28 a small 1 party of foragers was picked up by 400 of the enemy, and 200 infantry and 80 cavalry, including Cos. D and M, started in pursuit. The cavalry dashed into the Confederates and scattered their pickets in every direction. Co. D dismounted and drove the enemy for some

distance.   The regiment was stationed at West Plains, Pilot
Knob, St. Genevieve and Cape Girardeau, successively, from Jan. 7
to May 31, 1863, and was engaged with the enemy at Chalk bluff in
March. At Whitewater bridge Capt. Shipman and 40 men on guard
were surrounded by 300 of the enemy, but they cut their way out
with a loss of 6 killed, 9 wounded and 10 taken prisoners.   The
regiment was in the battle of Cape Girardeau, where it supported a
battery, and pursued the enemy in his retreat.   In June it was ordered
to join the cavalry corps of the Army of the Cumberland.   It reached
Nashville June 15, took part in the movement toward Chattanooga,
and was   stationed at various points during the summer.   It
participated at Chickamauga, where it was engaged with the cavalry
in holding the extreme right on the second day,   and covered the
retreat of the army.   It was in a lively engagement near Anderson's
gap in October, routing Wheeler's command and taking numerous
prisoners, and it was also in a skirmish at Maysville, Ala.   It then
marched to   Winchester, Alexandria   and New Market, Tenn.,
engaging the enemy at the last named place and driving him across
Mossy creek.   In this action the regiment carried the enemy's position
and captured a number of prisoners.   In December it again repulsed
a force which had advanced on Mossy creek, and it participated in
the battle at Dandridge in Jan., 1864.   It was also in the engagement
near Sevierville, and was then stationed at Marysyille, Motley's ford,
Madisonville and Cleveland until May 3.   It was in a severe
engagement near Varnell's station with Wheeler's forces, was in the
advance on Dallas, and as skirmishers, was under a fierce fire from
the enemy's batteries intrenched in a spur of the Allatoona hills, being
forced to fall back. A detachment under Capt. Comstock routed a
force at Burnt Hickory, and held its position against the attack of a
body of cavalry until reinforced. A battalion under Capt. Harnden
charged a heavy Confederate force guarding a supply train, and forced
a way through the enemy's ranks, but was compelled to fall back to
the reserves, where the enemy was checked. This dash has been
referred to as the most brilliant of the campaign. A detachment
defeated a force at Acworth and occupied the place. A few days later
the regiment was in a skirmish at Big Shanty, and it was in frequent
engagements about Lost mountain until the enemy's retreat across

the Chattahoochee river. It acted as part of McCook's expedition to the rear of Atlanta; attacked Armstrong's forces, 2,000 strong, near Campbell-ton, but was forced to retire. It moved to Marietta and from there to Cartersville, Ga., reaching the latter place on Aug. 12 and remaining there until Oct. 17, when it moved to Calhoun, thence to St. Louis to be remounted, reaching there Nov. 9. It left St. Louis Dec. 4 for Nashville and assisted in driving 2,000 of the enemy from Hopkinsville after a severe engagement. At Elizabethtown, Ky., Col. LaGrange with 20 men attacked a force of 400 and captured several prisoners. The regiments reached Nashville Jan. 5, 1865, then moved to Waterloo, Ala., and joined Wilson's cavalry expedition. The 1st Wis. cavalry was in the front ranks in a desperate assault upon a fort overlooking West Point, which was captured in a hand-to-hand struggle. On May 6 a detachment of the regiment under Lieut.-Col. Harnden set out to search for Jefferson Davis. At midnight of the 7th a negro gave a minute account of the whereabouts of Davis and at early dawn of the 8th Harnden set out, traveling 45 miles that day. Early on the 9th the detachment resumed the march and at Abbeville met Col. Pritchard of the 4th Mich. cavalry, who had been ordered to camp there, guard the ferry and patrol the river. At 3 o'clock next morning Harnden went forward, believing Davis to be near. The advance guard came upon armed men, who ordered them to halt, and opened fire. Harnden advanced with a large force and the firing became general until a prisoner captured by Sergt. Howe stated that the supposed enemy were Michigan troops under Col. Pritchard, who had selected his best mounted men after Harnden had frankly told him his mission and where Davis was supposed to be, and had proceeded at full speed to that point and surrounded the camp which held Davis, though the latter was not captured until after the regiments had fired upon each other. Many will ever believe the 1st Wis. cavalry entitled to at least equal credit for the capture. The regiment was stationed at Macon, Ga., until May 24 and was mustered out at Nashville July 19, 1865. Its original strength was 1,124. Gain by recruits, 1,056; substitutes, 83; draft, 278; veteran reenlistments, 61; total, 2,602. Loss by death, 366; desertion, 91; transfer, 67; discharge, 634; mustered out 1,444.

SECOND CAVALRY

Cols., Cadwallader C. Washburn, Thomas Stephens, Nicholas H. Dale; Lieut.-Cols., Thomas Stephens, Levi Sterling, William H. Miller, H. Eugene Eastman, Nicholas H. Dale, William Woods, Newton De Forest; Majs., William H. Miller, Nicholas H. Dale, Myron W. Wood, H. Eugene Eastman, William Woods, John Whytock, Edwin Skewes, Levi Sterling, Edward D. Luxton, George N. Richmond, Newton De Forest, George W. Ring. This regiment was organized at Camp Washburn, Milwaukee, between Dec. 3, 1861, and March 12, 1862. It left the state March 24 for Benton barracks, St. Louis, where it was mounted and equipped and was ordered to Springfield in May. The 2nd and 3d battalions were sent to join Gen. Curtis' army at Augusta, Ark., from there to Helena, where they remained until Jan., 1863, when they moved to Memphis, and in June to Snyder's bluff, Miss., where they remained during the siege of Vicksburg. They joined Sherman's expedition to Jackson in July and then returned to Redbone, 10 miles from Vicksburg. The 1st battalion was stationed at Springfield and Cassville, Mo., alternately until Oct., 1862, when it went to Osage Springs, Ark., and remained there until December. It was stationed at Forsyth, Mo., until the latter part of March, 1863, going from there to Lake Springs, and in Sept., 1864, joined the other battalions at Vicksburg. The regiment was on picket duty until Nov. 6, when it joined an expedition to Gaines' landing, Ark. Subsequently it made a 300-mile expedition, destroying bridges, railroad track, cotton and supplies, and a detachment of 240 men engaged a considerable force of the enemy near Yazoo City. The regiment was ordered to Memphis on Dec. 10 and joined an expedition under Gen. Grierson into Mississippi, destroying much railroad property, bridges and stores, defeating the enemy in a severe action at Egypt Station and capturing 500 prisoners, who were placed in charge of the 2nd. The command then marched through to Vicksburg, destroying the enemy's line of communication, then returned to Memphis and soon after made two similar expeditions without notable incident. On May 9, 1865, a detachment of 330 was sent to Grenada, Miss., for garrison duty and remained until June 24, when it rejoined the regiment at Alexandria, La. It was assigned to the 2nd brigade, 2nd cavalry division, Department of the Gulf, and marched to Hemstead, Tex., where it went into camp. It was mustered out at Austin, Tex., Nov. 15, 1865. Its original strength was 1,127. Gain by recruits, 979; substitutes, 18; draft, 1; veteran reenlistments, 385; total, 2,510. Loss by death, 271; missing, 1; desertion, 103; transfer, 33; discharge, 557; mustered out, 1,541.

THIRD CAVALRY

Cols., William A. Barstow, Thomas Derry; Lieut.-Cols., Richard H. White, Elias A. Calkins, David S. Vittam, Theodore Conkey; Majs., Elias A. Calkins, Thomas Derry, Lorenzo B. Reed, Benjamin S. Henning, William Culbertson, John C. Schroeling, James B. Pond. This regiment was organized at Camp Barstow, Janesville, and was mustered in at various dates from Nov. 30, 1861, to Jan. 31, 1862. It left the state March 26, 1862, for St. Louis, and 12 men were killed and 28 injured in a railway accident near Chicago while en route. The regiment was sent to Leavenworth May 22, Col. Barstow being appointed provost marshal-general of Kansas. Cos. C, F, I and M were ordered to Port Scott June 12, under the command of Maj. Henning, who took charge of the post. Bushwhackers and roving bands of guerrillas were speedily driven from that vicinity which was an outpost. Co. I was sent to Carthage, Mo., to protect loyalists, disperse guerrillas and keep watch on the enemy, and Co. C went to Trading Post for similar duty. Upon learning that a large force of the enemy was concentrating near Montevallo, Mo., Co. I was ordered to march from Carthage to meet forces from Fort Scott in an attack. Reaching the point in advance of the troops from Port Scott, Co. I, under Capt. Conkey, charged through the camp of the enemy, 2,000 strong, and pushed on, but missed Col. Barstow, who was leading the approaching troops by another road. The company proceeded to Montevallo, where it engaged in a skirmish, and then started for Fort Scott, but was attacked by a greatly superior body of the enemy and escaped with a loss of 4 men captured. Cos. F and I accompanied an expedition in pursuit of the enemy in August and Co. I had the front at Taberville, being especially mentioned for gallantry in the official report. Cos. C and F were detached in September and employed until Jan., 1863, in scout and train guard duty, Cos. I and M replacing them at the fort. C and G made a part of the garrison until July. In the assignment in June of the previous year, Co. D was sent to Atchison, Co. G to Shawnee, Co. L to Aubrey, Cos. B and H to post duty at Fort Leavenworth, and Cos. A, E and K to provost duty in the city of Leavenworth. The last three were also engaged in scouting expeditions through the border counties of Missouri and on Sept. 13, six companies were attached to the 1st brigade, Army of Missouri and sent to Indian creek in southwest Missouri. They took part in the battles of Cane Hill and Prairie Grove, were ordered to Fort Scott the following June, and reached there July 5. On May 30 Cos. B, G, H, I and M, while on escort duty, repulsed 1,500 Texans and Indians with heavy loss to the enemy, and in June, as part of an escort of 1,000 men, they defeated a greatly superior force, driving it 50 miles across the country. Arriving at Fort Blunt, their destination, these companies were attached to the 3d brigade, Army of the Frontier, and took part in the battle of Honey Springs. They were engaged in scouting and skirmishing most of the summer and fall, were joined at Van Buren, Ark., in October by Cos. E and K and the detachment routed a superior force at Waldron. The following day it put a large force of Indians to flight and it defeated a force of 1,000 in the Mulberry mountains in November. These seven companies were stationed at Van Buren from Nov., 1863, to Feb., 1864, on escort and guard duty. Co. I, while serving as escort to Gen. Blunt in Oct., 1863, was attacked by 500 of Quantrill's band. It made a gallant resistance, which secured the safety of the commanding general, but it was compelled to retreat with a loss of 22 killed, and 4 wounded, the most serious loss any com-pany in the regiment sustained. In Jan., 1864, three-fourths of the regiment reenlisted and after a furlough were sent to Benton barracks. The regiment was ordered to Memphis in July and sent to Devall's Bluff, Ark. It engaged in picket duty and scouting service in the vicinity of Huntersville and Little Rock most of the time until Aug. 28. A detachment under Maj. Derry, with other mounted troops, numbering 800 in all, routed a body of 1,200 cavalry, and 145 men under Maj. Derry took part in an expedition to Fort Smith in September. The remaining companies were stationed at various points in Missouri, except Co. M. which was sent to Pawnee, Kan. Most of the regiment remained near Little Rock during the winter, engaged in scout, guard, patrol and skirmish duty. The regiment was reorganized April 19, 1865, and, that part which was stationed at Little Rock was consolidated into Cos. A, B, C, D and E, this battalion leaving for St. Louis on April 21. From there it went to Springfield, Mo., for post duty, and was mustered out at Fort Leavenworth, Sept. 8, 1865. The remaining companies performed the usual scout, guard and forage duty during the summer, F, H, I and K being mustered out Sept. 29, and G and L Oct. 27 and 23 respectively. The original strength of the regiment was 1,186. Gain by recruits, 962; substitutes, 18; veteran reenlist-ments, 357; total, 2,523. Loss by death, 215; missing, 9; desertion, 126; transfer, 64; discharge, 418; mustered out, 1,691.

FOURTH CAVALRY

See the 4th Infantry, organized as such, but later mounted and attached to the cavalry service.

MILWAUKEE CAVALRY

Capt., Gustav von Deutsch; First-Lieut., Charles Lehman; Second Lieuts., Louis Pelosi, Albert Galoskowsky. This company was organized at Milwaukee in July and Aug., 1861, and left the state in September, being mustered in at St. Louis Sept. 23, as an independent body. It served for a short time as body-guard to Gen. Fremont, and was then incorporated as Co. M, with the 4th Mo. cavalry, with which it served until mustered out. Its original strength was 83. Gain by recruits, 1; veteran reenlistments, 9; total, 93.

FIRST LIGHT BATTERY

Capts., Jacob T. Foster, Daniel Webster. First Lieuts., Alexander Cameron, Daniel Webster, Oscar F. Nutting, John D. Anderson, Charles B. Kimball; Second Lieuts., Albert W. Bishop, Charles B. Kimball, Oscar F. Nutting, Ephraim L. Hackett, Edward P. Aylmer, Edwin E. Stewart. This battery was organized at La Crosse in Sept.,

1861, and was mustered in Oct. 10.   It rendezvoused at Racine from early October until Jan. 23, 1862, when it left the state. It encamped at St. Louis until April 3 and then joined Gen. Morgan's expedition to Cumberland gap, hauling the Parrott guns by hand over the steep passes.   In August it assisted in repulsing the enemy in a fight at Tazewell; assisted in the defense of Cumberland gap until Sept. 17, and then joined the forces under Gen. Fox in Virginia.   In Dec., 1862, it joined Sherman's forces at Memphis and started toward Vicksburg. It did effective work at Chickasaw bluffs and also in the reduction of Arkansas Post, where the work of the right section of the battery won from Gen. Osterhaus this praise: "The reduction of the lower casemate (of the fort) and the silencing of 3 or 4 formidable guns are their exclusive merit."   It remained at and about Vicksburg until spring and at the battle of Port Gibson it dismounted 4 of the enemy's guns and cut to pieces the celebrated Virginia battery, its fire being most effective.   It participated at Champion's hill; was engaged at the Big Black river the following day; bore a prominent part in the first assault at Vicksburg, doing terrible execution; and continued to perform excellent service during the entire siege. During the Vicksburg campaign the battery fired over   12,000 rounds, its   20-pounder Parrotts becoming so worn as to be unserviceable and were replaced with 30-pounders. After the fall of Vicksburg it aided in the reduction of Jackson.   The battery was attached to the 13th army corps, Department of the Gulf, and in December, joined the forces at New Orleans, where it was equipped as horse artillery.   An inspecting committee said of it: "A more self-sustaining, self-reliant body of men cannot be found in the U. S. Army." It covered Banks' retreat in the Red River expedition in April, 1864, and was in the engagement at Alexandria in May.   In October 80 of the battery, whose term of service had expired, left for home, their places being filled by reenlistments and recruits.   Capt. Foster was commissioned lieutenant-colonel of the 1st Wis. heavy artillery, and Lieut. Webster was advanced to the captaincy.   On Nov. 26 the battery accompanied a cavalry expedition to West Pascagoula, Miss., but returned to New Orleans and Baton Rouge and remained there until ordered home.   It was mustered out at Milwaukee July 7, 1865.   Its original strength was 155.   Gain by recruits, 112; substitutes, 2; reenlistments, 34; total, 303. Loss by death, 22; desertion, 7; transfer, 14; discharge, 48; mustered out, 212.

SECOND LIGHT BATTERY

Capts., Ernst F. Hersberg, Charles Berger; First Lieuts., J. C. Her von Schlen, Charles Berger, John Bulander, Charles Schulz, Charles Saupe, C. J. Emil Stephan, John Schabel, Lewis Rabe; Second Lieuts., John Schabel, Charles Schulz, August Buchwald, Charles Saupe, Edward Hanson, Charles Berger, John Bulander, George Fischer. This battery, known as the "Washington Artillery," was organized at Camp Utley, Racine, in Sept. 1861, and was mustered in Oct. 10. It left the state Jan. 21, 1862 for Baltimore, thence to Washington, and was ordered to Fortess Monroe as part of the garrison, remaining there until September. It then moved to Camp Hamilton, Va., for garrison duty and on Jan. 10, 1863, was sent to Suffolk, Va. In January 5 pieces of the battery engaged in the battle near South Mary bridge. During March and April, 3 pieces of the battery were stationed between Forts Dix and Union, and 2 pieces on the Nansemond river. On May 6 the battery was ordered to Portsmouth, from there to West Point and thence to Williamsburg, where it remained until July 20. It then moved to Yorktown, where it was retained until Jan. 20, 1864, and then proceeded to Point Lookout, Md., where it was employed principally as guard for prisoners until mustered out. Its original strength was 153. Gain by recruits, 42; reenlisted veterans, 48; total, 243. Loss by death, 12; desertion, 6; transfer, 7; discharge, 30; mustered out, 188.

THIRD LIGHT BATTERY

Capt., Lucius H. Drury; First Lieuts., Cortland Livingston, Hiram F. Hubbard, James T. Purdy, Henry Currier; Second Lieuts., Albert Le Brun, Henry Currier, Webster J. Colburn, Joseph W. Wait, Hiram F. Hubbard. This battery, known as the "Badger Artillery," was organized at Camp Utley, Racine, in Sept. and Oct., 1861. It was mustered in Oct. 10, and left the state Jan. 23, 1862, for Louisville, Ky., where it was armed with rifled 32-pounders. It went into camp at Nashville

March 14, joined Grant at Savannah, Tenn., April 3, and moved to Pittsburg landing. It was on the march through Mississippi, Alabama, Tennessee and Kentucky during the summer, and was present at Perryville, but not in action. It accompanied the army in the southward movement, having several small engagements, and was stationed for a time at Mount Vernon, Ky. It was in camp at Nashville until Dec. 26 and then accompanied the army in the movement towards Murfreesboro. It was in action at Stone's river, where it guarded a ford and repelled a charge of cavalry upon a hospital. On New Year's day, 1863, with a brigade of infantry, it crossed the river, fired a few rounds at the enemy's skirmishers and cavalry, and received a strong fire in return. It advanced in the afternoon and developed the opposing army stationed in the woods, but was compelled to fall back across the river, when it was reinforced and the enemy was routed. In Jan., 1863, Capt. Drury was appointed chief of artillery on Gen. Van Cleve's staff. The battery encamped near Murfreesboro until July 5, then went to McMinnville and engaged in scout and picket duty. It participated at the battle of Chickamauga, where it was overwhelmed by numbers and driven from the field, losing 5 of its 6 guns, 33 horses and 26 men killed, wounded and missing. It was stationed at Chattanooga during 1864, on guard and garrison duty, and was transferred to Murfreesboro in the spring of 1865. It was mustered out at Madison, July 20, 1865. Its original strength was 170. Gain by recruits, 100; total, 270. Loss by death, 26; deser-tion, 3; transfer, 4; discharge, 60; mustered out, 177.

Fourth Light Battery

Capts., John F. Vallee, George B. Easterly, Dorman L. Noggle; First Lieuts,, John F. Valee, George B. Easterly, Martin H. McDevitt, William P. Powers, Burr Maxwell, Spencer S. Hillier, Dorman L. Noggle, Robert Campbell; Second Lieuts., Andrew H. Hunt, Charles A. Rathbun, George R. Wright, Dorman L. Noggle, Burr Maxwell, Delos H. Cady, Martin H. McDevitt, Alexander See, George R. Wright, Dorman L. Noggle, Levi Westinghouse, Robert Campbell, Benjamin Brown. This battery was organized at Beloit, Sept. 14, 1861, and was sent to Camp Utley, Racine, Sept. 19. It was mustered in Oct. 1 and left the state Jan. 21, 1862, for Washington, but was sent at once to Fortress Monroe, where it was put in charge of the barbette guns and spent the summer. It had the honor of firing the gun "Union" during the engagement between the Monitor and Merrimac. When fully equipped it was sent to Camp Hamilton near Hampton, Va., and was engaged there in garrison duty until Jan. 11, '863. It was then ordered to Suffolk and assisted in the defense against Longstreet during April. It was at West Point during May, constructing fortifications, and joined Keyes' expedition toward Richmond in June, a junction with Dix's forces being effected on the 29th. The battery went into camp at Yorktown July 10, was ordered to Gloucester Point Aug. 25, and remained there until Oct. 11, when it was attached to Getty's command at Portsmouth for permanent duty. It engaged in small expeditions and reconnoissances until April 23, 1864, when it was assigned to the artillery brigade, 1st division, 18th army corps, which moved up the James river and took part in the two days engagements about Fort Clinton on the Appomattox. It was under fire at Proctor's creek, near Drewry's bluff and covered the army's rear as it retired. It took position in the intrenchments on Bermuda Hundred, where it remained until June 4, when it was attached to Kautz's cavalry division, with which it participated in the early assaults on Petersburg, at one time being exposed for 2 hours to a concentrated fire of 14 guns. On July 8 the entire battery was converted into horse artillery and on the 27th the left section moved with the cavalry and participated in the battle of Malvern hill. The right section made a short expedition at the same time to Lighthouse point on the James and on Aug. 4 went to Prince George Court House. The battery returned to Petersburg and was in numerous engagements with the Army of the Potomac in and about Richmond. It was mustered out July 3, 1865. Its original strength was 151. Gain by recruits, 62; substitutes, 38; reenlistments, 43; total, 294. Loss by death, 24; missing, 1; desertion, 15; transfer, 1; discharge, 82; mustered out, 171.

FIFTH LIGHT BATTERY

Capts., Oscar F. Pinney, Charles B. Humphrey, George Q. Gardner, Joseph McKnight; First Lieuts., Washington Hill, George Q. Gardner,

Joseph McKnight, George Lafferty, Daniel Titus, Charles B. Humphrey, Elijah Booth, Jr.; Second Lieuts., Almon Smith, Joseph McKnight, George Lafferty, Daniel Titus, Elijah Booth Jr., John Dickinson, George Q. Gardner, Charles M. Wyman. This battery was organized at Monroe, but afterwards rendezvoused at Camp Utley, Racine, and was mustered in Oct. 1, 1861. It left the state March 15, 1862, for St. Louis and was ordered to New Madrid, where it was engaged in building and guarding forts until the surrender of Island No. 10. It moved with Pope's army in April, took position near Corinth, and was in the battle of Farmington, where two sections of the battery took position in the extreme front and for three days defended a bridge, across which the enemy must advance. The battery passed through the siege of Corinth, was then on guard duty at Ripley from June 29 until Aug. 14, when it was transferred to the Army of the Tennessee and marched to Nashville, thence to Louisville, skirmished with the enemy at Bardstown and participated in the battle of Perryville. It supported McCook's corps, which was hard pressed, and repelled three attempts to take the battery. Gen. McCook thanked the battery, saying it had "saved the corps from disgraceful defeat." It was engaged at Stone's river, where it checked the enemy's advance and was again commended for its "gallant and distinguished" service. It encamped at Murfreesboro during the winter and spring of 1863, and joined the advance towards Chattanooga in June. It reached Crawfish springs at Chickamauga on the second day of the battle, but was not in action. It remained near Chickamauga until Nov. 20, going out on short expeditions. Most of the men reenlisted in Jan., 1864, and were furloughed home for a month. On their return the battery was assigned to the 2nd division, 14th army corps, near Rossville, Ga. It was actively engaged at Resaca and was in a severe skirmish near Rome a few days later. It held several important positions in the operations about Dallas, and was in the front at Kennesaw mountain. Subsequently it took a new position from which it did such effective work as to compel the enemy's artillery to vacate its position. At the battle of Peachtree creek it shelled the enemy out of his works and was then in active service about Atlanta until Aug. 28. It was in the engagement at Jonesboro, and then remained in camp at Atlanta until Oct. 3, when it went on the expedition to repel

Hood's threatened attack upon the railroad communications. It returned to Atlanta, moved from there to Savannah with the army, accompanied Sherman north, participated in the battle of Bentonville, and the review at Washington. It was mustered out at Madison June 14, 1865. Its original strength was 155. Gain by recruits, 70; reenlistments, 79; total, 304. Loss by death, 24; deser-tion, 1; transfer, 5; discharge, 61; mustered out, 213.

SIXTH LIGHT BATTERY

Capts., Henry Dillon, Thomas R. Hood, James G. Simpson; First Lieuts., Henry Dillon, Samuel F. Clark, John Jenawein, Thomas R. Hood, Alba S. Sweet; Second Lieuts., John W. Fancher, James G. Simpson, Sylvester E. Sweet. Daniel T. Noyes, John Jenawein, Lucius N. Keller. This battery, known as the "Buena Vista Artillery," was organized at Lone Rock in Sept., 1861, but was transferred to Camp Utley, Racine, where it was mustered in Oct. 2, and left the state March 15, 1862. It reported at St. Louis, was ordered to New Madrid, and placed in charge of a battery during the siege of Island No. 10. It was in reserve during the siege of Corinth, but took part in the battle in October. It spent the winter in Tennessee, joined the movement toward Vicksburg in the spring of 1863, went to Helena and was sent out on several minor expeditions. It participated at Port Gibson; was in a sharp skirmish at Jones' cross-roads; was at the battle of Raymond in reserve; took part in the battle of Jackson; was engaged at Champion's hill, and was in the trenches before Vicksburg from May 19 until the surrender. It remained at Vicksburg until Sept. 12, then moved to Chattanooga and was in the battle at Missionary ridge. It was then on railroad guard duty until Jan. 7, 1864. It wintered at Huntsville, Ala., and spent the summer on the Etowah river near Cartersville, Ga., most of the time in Fort Etowah. On Nov. 10 it left for Nashville and joined the reserve battery at Fort Barry. On Jan. 7, 1865, it was transferred to the reserve garrison artillery. The men were armed with muskets on Jan. 16 and assigned to provost guard duty. On Feb. 17 it was sent to a permanent camp at Chattanooga and was mustered out at Madison July 18, 1865. Its original strength was 157. Gain by recruits, 82; substitutes, 2; reenlistments, 34; total, 275.

Loss by death, 29; desertion, 5; transfer, 9; discharge, 36; mustered out, 196.

SEVENTH LIGHT BATTERY

Capts., Richard R. Griffith, Harry S. Lee, Arthur B. Wheelock; First Lieuts., Harry S. Lee, Galen E. Green, Arthur B. Wheelock, William E. Hearsey, James H. Bridgeman; Second Lieuts., Arthur B. Wheelock, William E. Hearsey, James H. Bridgeman, Moses Jerome, Samuel Hayes, Frank Fox, James H. Langworthy. This battery, called the "Badger State Flying Artillery," was organized at Milwaukee during the summer and fall of 1861, and was mustered in Oct. 4. It left the state March 15, 1862, for St. Louis and was sent to New Madrid, where it was placed in charge of heavy siege guns during the siege of Island No. 10. It was engaged in garrison duty on that island after its surrender and on June 11, left for Union City and Trenton, Tenn., for railroad guard duty. On July 20 it moved to Humboldt and remained there until Dec. 1, when the battery was divided, 3 guns being sent to Trenton. About the middle of the month, a feint by Forrest's cavalry on Jackson led to a concentration of forces at that point, leaving a part of the battery, some horses, camp and garrison equipage, all of which was captured by the enemy two days later, as well as much of the camp equipage at Trenton. Half of the battery was sent as far as Lexington, Ky., after Forrest and the entire battery took part at Parker's cross-roads in December, but the enemy with 10 guns in concentric fire disabled the guns of one section and captured the men handling them. Most of those captured were released later by a charge of infantry. The battery was stationed at Jackson until June 1, 1863, when it moved to Corinth, thence to Memphis, where it was attached to the 4th brigade, 5th division, 16th army corps, for permanent garrison duty, and remained there, with the exception of a few short expeditions, until the close of the war. The reenlisted veterans took a furlough home in February, but returned early in April, and on May 1 the right section joined the pursuit of Forrest, a ten days hard trip. The left section engaged in a similar expedition in June and in a severe engagement near Gun town, Miss., lost its guns, and 5 men. The guns were soon retaken and used on the

99

raiders with telling effect. The battery was mustered out at Madison. Its original strength was 158. Gain by recruits, 93; substitutes, 1; reenlistments, 92; total, 344. Loss by death, 29; desertion, 9; transfer, 1; discharge, 68; mustered out, 237.

EIGHTH LIGHT BATTERY

Capts., Stephen J. Carpenter, Henry E. Stiles; First Lieuts., James E. Armstrong, George L. Cross, Obadiah German, Henry E. Stiles, John D. McLean, Thomas B. McNair; Second Lieuts., John D. McLean, Henry L. Wheeler, Azro Mann, Samuel S. Armstrong, Thomas B. McNair, William O'D Reilly. This battery, known as "Lyon's Pinery Battery," was organized in the fall of 1861 at Stevens Point.   It rendezvoused at Camp Utley, Racine, was mustered in Jan. 8, 1862, and left the state March 18 for St. Louis.   On April 4 it proceeded to Fort Leavenworth to join the Southwestern expedition. At Fort Riley it was ordered to Columbus, Ky., and thence to Humboldt, Tenn., for guard duty.   In July it was ordered to Mississippi and reached Corinth on the 9th.   It was next transferred to the army of the Tennessee, and two sections were sent to Nashville, the center section under Lieut. McLean being left at Eastport, Miss.   The other two sections were in the battle of Perryville, afterward joining in the pursuit of the enemy and shelling him from his position at Lancaster. They then returned to Nashville.   The center section left Eastport for Iuka, but did not reach there in time for the battle.   At Corinth it did excellent work and was ranked with those who greatly distinguished themselves.   It joined the right and left sections at Nashville and at Stone's river the battery performed honorable service. It encamped at Murfreesboro during the winter and spring of 1863, and was in action at Chickamauga.   It was also in action at Missionary ridge and Lookout mountain, and was ordered to Nashville in December, where it was assigned to the 2nd division, artillery reserve. The veterans were remustered, Jan. 26, 1864, and given a furlough. They rejoined the battery at Murfreesboro in April, and it was assigned to Fort Rosecrans for garrison duty.   It was mustered out at Milwaukee, Aug. 10, 1865. Its original strength was 161.   Gain by recruits, 102; reenlistments, 66; total, 329.   Loss by death, 25;

missing, 1; desertion, 13; transfer, 14; discharge, 53; mustered out, 223.

NINTH LIGHT BATTERY

Capts., Cyrus H. Johnson, James H. Dodge, Watson D. Crocker; First Lieuts., James H. Dodge, Watson D. Crocker, John A. Edington; Second Lieuts., John A. Edington, Henry A. Hicks, Albert Helliwell. This battery, known as the Randall Battery, was organized and mustered into service on Jan. 27, 1862. It remained at Racine until March 18, when it proceeded in company with the 8th and 10th batteries to St. Louis. On April 3 it embarked for Leavenworth, Kan., where it prepared for a march across the plains. On the 26th it proceeded by way of Fort Kearny and Julesburg, to Denver, reaching there on June 2 after a march of 700 miles. On June 4 it proceeded to Fort Union, New Mex., and soon afterward Lieut. Crocker with the left section marched to Fort Larned and remained there until Dec., 1864. On July 5, the right section marched to Fort Lyon, where it joined the center section. These two sections remained in Colorado until April 26, 1864, either at the fort or at Denver, making frequent marches to the distant frontier. The most noteworthy of these was made by Lieut. Edington with one section in June, 1863. The march was a distance of 240 miles and it was made in three days—the quickest in the history of the war at that date. In April, 1864, the battery marched to Council Grove, Kan., where it remained as garrison of the town, escorting trains and U. S. mail coaches over the road until August, when it went to Fort Riley. In July Lieut. Edington with one section joined in an expedition against the Indians at Fort Larned. Late in August he joined an expedition to Smoky Hill, where the Indians were defeated in a well contested engagement. In July, 1863, Lieut. Crocker and the left section held Fort Larned with its large and valuable government supplies against the combined forces of the Indians in that locality. In Oct., 1864, Capt. Dodge, with 4 guns, joined the command of Gen. Curtis and participated in the campaign against Price in Missouri and Arkansas. In the battle at Westport the battery broke the charge of a column, 6,000 strong, three successive times. In Dec. 1864, this portion of the battery proceeded to Fort

Leavenworth, where soon afterward it was joined by the other detachments preparatory to reorganization of the veterans. The aggregate distance marched by the battery and detached section during these three years was nearly 15,000 miles. The veteran battery was organized Jan. 27, 1865, with Lieut. Crocker as Captain. On March 26 Lieut. Edington with one section marched to Fort Scott and remained there until June 16, when he pro-ceeded to Fort Riley. This section left Fort Riley for western Kansas and was mustered out at Fort Leavenworth Sept. 30. The original strength of the battery was 155. Gain by recruits, 63; reenlistments, 78; total, 296. Loss by death, 6; transfer, 1; discharge, 56; mustered out, 233.

Tenth Light Battery

Capt., Yates V. Beebe; First Lieuts., David C. Pratt, Philip H. M. Groesbeck, Ebenezer W. Stetson; Second Lieuts., Philip H. M. Groesbeck, Elbert W. Fowler, Henry A. Hicks, Oscar A. Clark. This battery was organized at New Lisbon in the fall of 1861, and was mustered in Feb. 10, 1862. It rendezvoused at Camp Utley, Racine, and left the state March 18 for St. Louis. On April 1, Lieut. Toner and 25 men were transferred to the 8th battery, and Lieut. Hicks and 45 men to the 9th, leaving but 47 men in the 10th. These were joined in April by 25 recruits and the battery was assigned to the reserve artillery at Pittsburg landing. It was in action at the siege of Corinth and then encamped at Tuscumbia creek until July 21, when it moved to Iuka and left there Aug. 12 to join the Army of the Tennessee near Nashville. One section, which had been left at Courtland, rejoined the battery at Decatur, Ala., in September. It routed a body of Van Dorn's cavalry at Columbia, Tenn., and upon reaching Nashville engaged in train escort service. In November its ranks were augmented by 50 recruits and on Dec. 12 it was assigned to the 2nd brigade, 7th division, 14th corps. It escorted a train to Murfreesboro, where it was temporarily detached and participated in the battle of Stone's river. It was on garrison duty at Nashville until April 8; on railroad guard duty at Brentwood until June 3; in garrison at Murfreesboro until Aug. 19; in camp at Athens, Ala., until Sept. 1; on bridge guard duty at and near Bridgeport, Tenn., until Oct. 10; and then guarded the river at various points until Jan. 1, 1864, when one section moved to Calhoun. It was joined by the other sections in February, and was employed as bridge guard until April 27, when it was ordered to Cleveland, Tenn., and assigned to the 3d cavalry division, Army of the Cumberland. It was heavily engaged at Resaca and Calhoun ferry being praised for its "energy, prompt maneuvering and accurate firing." It was on guard duty in the vicinity of Adairsville, Kingston and Cartersville until Aug. 3, and at Red Oak it silenced the enemy's battery and destroyed 2 miles of railroad. It engaged a battery at Jonesboro with the same result, burned the depot, rolling stock and buildings, and destroyed 3 miles of track. It made a vigorous attack on the enemy at Lovejoy's Station and a few days later again silenced the battery at Red Oak. It was in lively engagements at Burnt bridge, Glass bridge, Salt Springs, Nose's creek and Rome, and then went into camp at Marietta. It participated in the march to the sea, taking part in engagements at Lovejoy's Station, Waynesboro, Buckhead Church and other points. It then joined in the campaign of the Carolinas, and was actively engaged at Barnwell, Aiken, Gunter's bridge, Hornsboro, Monroe's crossing and Averasboro. The non-veterans who were entitled to discharge, were mustered out at Madison, April 26, 1865, and the balance of the battery was temporarily attached to the 12th Wis. battery. The original strength of the 10th was 47; recruits, 121; reenlistments, 11; total, 179. Loss by death, 24; desertion, 4; discharge, 60; mustered out, 91.

ELEVENTH LIGHT BATTERY

Capt., John Rourke; First Lieuts., John McAfee, Carles Bagley; Second Lieuts., William L. McKenzie, Michael Lantry, Michael Cunningham. This battery was known as the "Oconto Irish Guards," and was organized for the 17th regiment at Oconto early in 1862. It was transferred to Col. Mulligan's "Irish Brigade," at Camp Douglas, Chicago, and left there on June 14, 1862. On the 23d it crossed the Potomac at Harpers Ferry and went into camp at New creek, W. Va. On Oct. 28 a section accompanied a cavalry force to intercept the enemy under Imboden at Greenland gap. Near Petersburg they overtook and skirmished with him. In November a large force with two sections of the battery engaged in a fight with the same enemy 18 miles beyond Moorefield. In April, 1863, they again encountered and drove Imboden, near Philippi. In the same month one section held Rowlesburg and one Fairmount, but the whole battery was soon forced to retire to New creek. In July it changed its position to Hedgeville, and thence to Petersburg and Moorefield, where in September one section repulsed two assaults of the enemy. In November the battery became associated with Gen. Averell's command and assisted in destroying the Virginia and Tennessee railroad. On Nov. 26, Lieut. McAfee and a detachment of 18 men participated in a march towards Moorefield, but encountered a superior force of the enemy and was forced to retreat. On Jan. 22, 1865, the battery reported at Harper's Ferry, where it remained till mustered out. Its original strength was 87. Gain by recruits, 8; reenlistments, 39; total, 134. Loss by death, 3; desertion, 20; transfer, 2; discharge, 17; mustered out, 92.

TWELFTH LIGHT BATTERY

Capts., William A. Pile, William Zickerick; First Lieuts., William Zickerick, Edward G. Harlow, William Miles, Lorenzo D. Immel, Marcus Amsden, Sylvester C. Cheney, Philander H. Cody; Second Lieuts., William H. Hamilton, Marcus Amsden, Samuel E. Jones, Philander H. Cody, Henry Marks, Sylvester C. Cheney, Henry Turner. This battery was organized in the winter of 1862 and was mustered in by squads during March, 1863. It was sent to Jefferson barracks, Mo., as mustered, with the understanding that it was to be attached to the 1st Mo. artillery as the 12th Wis. battery. Capt. Pile, a Missourian, who had been given special authority by Gov. Harvey to recruit the battery, refused to acknowledge Gov. Harvey's authority after leaving the state and proceeded to distribute the men according to his own pleasure. On July 18 the governor revoked his commission with the approval of the war department, William Zickerick succeeding him. A number of the recruits were temporarily attached to a Missouri battery in March, pending the completion of the battery's organization, and were engaged in the siege of Island No. 10. In May two sections of the battery joined Halleck's forces before Corinth, whither the other section had preceded them, and on the 29th one section, under Lieut. Zickerick, destroyed a redoubt commanding a railroad. The battery joined in pursuit of the enemy, then camped at Clear creek and remained in that vicinity until August. It was then at Jacinto, Miss., until Oct. 1, though it took part in the battle of Iuka in September, and in the meantime was reinforced by 71 recruits. It was engaged at Corinth in October and was on garrison duty there until Nov. 8. It was then in the movement through Mississippi and Tennessee until Jan. 4, 1863, when it was assigned to guard duty near Germantown. It was in camp at Memphis from Feb. 8 to March 1, then moved toward Vicksburg and took part in the "Yazoo Pass" expedition. In the campaign in the rear of Vicksburg it was in action at Port Gibson, Raymond and Champion's hill, and was then engaged in the siege of Vicksburg until the surrender. It then engaged in various movements through Mississippi, Tennessee and Alabama until Jan. 9, 1864, when it was placed on garrison duty at Huntsville. In June it was then ordered to Kingston, Ga., thence to Allatoona on garrison duty, and was active in the celebrated defense of Allatoona in October. It was with Sherman on the march to the sea and on Jan. 14, 1865, moved to Beaufort, S. C., thence to Columbia, and on to Goldsboro. In April it went into camp, 4 miles from Raleigh, and left there on the 29th for Washington, where it participated in the grand review. It was mustered out at Madison, June 26, 1865. Its original strength was 99. Gain by recruits, 209; substitutes, 3; reenlistments, 31; total, 342. Loss by death, 30; missing, 1; desertion, 2; transfer, 81; discharge, 105; mustered out, 123.

THIRTEENTH LIGHT BATTERY

Capt., Richard R. Griffith; First Lieuts., George L. Cross, Alfred E. Chafiee, William W. Perrine, William M. Bristol; Second Lieuts., William W. Perrine, William M. Bristol, Frank Fox, David Kinder. This battery was organized in the fall of 1863 at Milwaukee. One squad was mustered in Nov. 4 and the other Dec. 29. The battery left the state Jan. 28, 1864, reached Memphis on Feb. 1, and New Orleans on the 12th. It was ordered to Baton Rouge and assigned to duty in Fort Williams, where it was placed in charge of 6 heavy guns. On

June 17 it was ordered to provost duty in the city of Baton Rouge, but returned to Fort Williams on July 8, taking charge of 7 barbette guns, and on the 10th was completely equipped as light artillery, taking the entire equipment of the 1st Vt. battery, whose term of service had expired. On the 15th it went into camp at Baton Rouge and remained there until ordered home. It was mustered out at Milwaukee, July 20, 1865. Its original strength was 156. Gain by recruits, 32; total, 188. Loss by death, 14; missing, 1; desertion, 25; transfer, 3; discharge, 39; mustered out, 106.

First Heavy Artillery

Col., Charles C. Meservey; Lieut.-Col., Jacob T. Foster; Majs., Charles C. Meservey, L. H. Drury, Richard W. Hubbell, David C. Fulton. Three days after the first battle of Bull Run (July 25, 1861), Co. K, 2nd Wis. infantry, was detached for garrison duty at Fort Corcoran near Washington. On Aug. 28 it occupied Fort Marcy and on Sept. 12, one-half of the company was ordered to Fort Ethan Allen for garrison and instruction duty. On Oct. 10 it rejoined the regiment, but on Dec. 9 was permanently detached and organized as an artillery company—the 1st battery Wis. heavy artillery— and stationed at Fort Cass. This formed the nucleus for Wisconsin's heavy artillery and on Aug. 28, 1862, a detachment of 40 men, with 3 pieces of artillery, was sent to garrison Fort Buffalo, an exposed post, where it repulsed an attack of the enemy. It returned to Fort Cass in September, moved to Fort Ellsworth in November, and was transferred to Fort Worth in May, 1863. In June Capt. Meservey was authorized to recruit a battalion of four batteries of heavy artillery, using the first battery as a basis. On Aug. 22 part of battery B was mustered in and by Sept. 9 was fully recruited. Battery A moved in October from Fort Worth to Battery Rodgers, where it remained until May, 1864. and was then transferred to Fort Willard. It returned to Battery Rodgers in August and was mustered out at Washington Aug, 18, 1865. Battery B left Milwaukee in Oct., 1863, was sent to Munfordville, Ky., and on Jan. 4, 1864, to Lexington, Ky., where it garrisoned Fort Clay until Aug. 30, 1865, when it was mustered out. Battery C was mustered in Oct. 1, 1863, left the state on the 30th, and was sent to Fort Wood,

Chattanooga. In Jan., 1864, it was sent to Fort Creighton and in May moved to Fort Sherman. On March 29, 1865, it moved to Athens, Tenn., and on April 5, marched to Mouse creek. On July 3 it was ordered to Strawberry plains, and was mustered out at Nashville Sept. 21, 1865. Battery D was mustered in Nov. 7, 1863; left the state Feb. 1, 1864, for New Orleans and was sent to Fort Jackson on garrison duty. In July it moved, to Fort Berwick, Brashear City, La., where it remained until June, 1865. It was mustered out Aug. 18, 1865. General orders No. 21, issued Sept. 14, 1864, called for the recruiting of eight additional companies to complete the regimental organization. Batteries L and M left the state, Sept. 30, E and F Oct. 3, H Oct. 7, K Oct. 17, and G and I Nov. 12. They were assigned to duty in the defenses at Washington as a part of the 4th brigade, De Russy's division, 22nd army corps, and remained at that point until mustered out Oct. 1, 1865. It is due the entire regiment to say that in discipline and appearance under arms, it was equal to any in the service. Its original strength was 1,777. Gain by recruits, 407; draft, 4; reenlistments, 29; total, 2,217. Loss by death, 73; desertion, 70; transfer, 28; discharge, 223; unaccounted for, 3; mustered out, 1,820.

ALL OTHER TROOPS

In addition to those previously enumerated, the records of the adjutant general for 1865 show the following credited to the state: Gibbon's brigade band, 15; Blunt's brigade band, 33; Colored troops, 244; army and navy, 714; out of state, 52; unassigned, 8,868. Quite a number of Indians were enrolled and performed valorous deeds.

INDEX

Ball, Farlin Q. 68
Ballard, Charles L. 76
Baltimore, MD 17, 37, 94
  Attack on Troops 9
Bank Riots 37
Banks, Nathaniel P. 36, 93
Bardstown, KY
  Skirmish at 97
Barnwell, SC
  Engagement at 103
Barre's Landing, LA 59
Barstow, William A. 17, 90
Bartlett, E. M. 67
Bartlett, James O. 44
Bashford, Coles 6
Baton Rouge, LA 37, 38, 60,
      93, 106
Battery Rodgers, VA 106
Bayfield, WI 67
Bayou Cache, AR
  Skirmish at 46
Bayou Lamourie, LA
  Battle of 44
Bayou Louis, LA 46
Beall, Samuel W. 53
Bean, Sidney A. 36
Beardsley, J. W. 29
Beaufort, SC 105
  Battle of 52
Beebe, Yates V. 102
Behrens, William F. 38
Belitz, Henry F. 80
Beloit Journal and Courier 14
Beloit, WI 10, 95
Benson, Ezzan H. 84
Benton Barracks, MO 56, 81, 82,
      86, 89, 91
Bentonville, NC
  Battle of 52, 53, 59, 63,
      69, 70, 98
Berdan, Hiram 84
Berdan's Sharpshooters 15
Berengaria 11
Berger, Charles 94
Bermuda Hundred, VA 96

Bertram, Henry 56
Beverly Ford, VA 41
Big Black River, MS 52
  Battle of 46, 49, 53, 59, 93
Big Piney, MO 82
Big Shanty, GA 87
Big Shanty, MS 47
Bigney, Thomas O. 48
Bill, George 41
Bingham, George B. 34
Bingham, James M. 77
Binnaker's Bridge, SC
  Battle of 70
Bintliff, James 76
Bird's Point, MO 50
Bishop, Albert W. 92
Bissell, Oliver C. 79
Black and White's Station, VA 41, 43
Black, Jeremiah S. 5
Blackford's Ford, VA 84
Blake, John W. 78
Bloodgood, Edward 58
Bloody Angle 42
Bloomfield, MO 86
Blunt, James 91
Blunt's Brigade Band 107
Boardman, Frederick A. 36
Boebel, Hans 62
Bolivar, MD 36
Bolivar, MS 53
Bolton, MS 47
Booth, Elijah, Jr. 97
Booth, Sherman M. 3, 4, 5
Botkins, W. Wallace 78
Bouck, Gabriel 53
Bovay, Alvin E. 5, 55
Bowling Green, KY 45, 61
Bracken, John 51
Bragg, Edward S. 39
Brandy Station, VA 85
  Battle of 36, 42
Brashear City, LA 37, 46, 60, 107
Brazos Santiago, TX 64
Brentwood, TN 58, 102
Bridgeman, James H. 99

110

Bridgeport, AL 54, 61
Bridgeport, TN 102
Brightman, Samuel B. 79
Britton, William B. 44
Brodhead, E. H. 11, 28
Brooks, Henry 37
Broome Co., NY 1
Brown, _____ (Mayor of
        Milwaukee) 10
Brown, Benjamin 95
Brown, John J. 64
Brownsville, AR 72, 73
Brownsville, TX 64, 65
Bryant, Edwin E. 82
Bryant, George E. 47
Bryant, Gustavus 66
Buchanan, James 5, 6
Buchwald, August 94
Buckhead Church, GA
    Engagement at 103
Buckland Mills, VA
    Battle of 42
Bugh, William A. 69
Bulander, John 94
Bull, James M. 38
Bull Run, VA
    Battle of 9, 27, 34, 35, 39,
        41, 106
    Second Battle of 84
Bureau of Employment for
        Discharged Soldiers 31
Burnt Bridge, GA
    Engagement at 103
Burnt Hickory, GA 87
Burrows, William S. 69
Butler, Benjamin 37
Butt, Cyrus M. 81
Buttrick, Edwin L. 60, 77
Buzzard Roost, GA 51

C

Cady, Delos H. 95
Cairo, Ill 69, 73, 78

Calhoun Ferry, GA
    Engagement at 103
Calhoun, GA 88
Calhoun, TN 103
Calkins, Elias A. 90
Callis, John B. 41
Calumet Co., WI 1
Camden (AR) Expedition 64
Camden, AR 64
Cameron, 16
Cameron, Alexander 92
Camp Barstow, WI 90
Camp Bragg, WI 57, 69
Camp, C. W. 12
Camp Douglas, IL 20, 103
Camp Fremont, WI 86
Camp Hamilton, VA 94, 96
Camp Harvey, WI 86
Camp Lyon, VA 39, 41
Camp Randall, WI 20, 39, 46, 47,
        50, 51, 52, 55, 56, 59, 66,
        67, 74, 75, 76, 77, 78, 79,
        80, 81, 82, 84
Camp Salomon, WI 61
Camp Sigel, WI 60, 62, 64
Camp Treadway, WI 48
Camp Utley, WI 55, 58, 68, 70, 94,
        95, 97, 98, 100, 102
Camp Washburn, WI
        73, 77, 81, 82, 89
Camp Wood, WI 49
Campbell, Robert 95
Cane Hill, AR 44
    Battle of 91
Cane River, LA
    Engagement on 72
Cape Fear River, NC
    Engagement on 70
Cape Girardeau, MO 64, 72, 86, 87
Carlton, Joseph H. 69
Carmargo Crossroads, MS 72
Carolinas Campaign 47, 52, 58, 62,
        63, 68, 70, 103
Carpenter, Matthew H. 10

Grant, Ulysses S. 95
Gravelly Run, VA
  Battle of 1, 43
Gray, Edmund B. 64
Greeley, Horace 5, 6
Green, Galen E. 99
Green, John 75
Green, Joseph E. 59
Green, Thomas H. 34
Greene, William A. 65
Greenland Gap, WV 103
Greenville, MO 86
  Battle of 44
Grenada, MS 89
Grier, Napoleon B. 67
Grierson, Benjamin 89
Griffith, Richard R. 99
Groesbeck, Philip H. M. 102
Gunter's Bridge, SC
  Engagement at 103
Guntown, MS
  Engagement at 99
Guppey, Joshua J. 45, 59

H

Habeas Corpus 3, 4, 5
Hackett, Ephraim L. 92
Halleck, Henry 104
Hamilton, Charles A. 41
Hamilton, Charles S. 36
Hamilton, William H. 74, 104
Hampton, VA 96
Hancock, Bradford 65
Hancock, John 49
Hancock, Winfield Scott 38, 42
Hanover Court House, VA
  Battle of 84
Hanson, Edward 94
Harkness, Robert 45
Harlow, Edward G. 104
Harnden, Henry 86, 87, 88
Harper's Ferry, WV 103, 104
Harriman, Samuel 75
Harris, Charles L. 34, 46

Harrisburg, PA 27
Harvey, Cordelia P. 30, 32
Harvey, L. P. 18, 19, 28, 30, 53, 104
Harvey United States Army General
  Hospital, WI 28, 31, 32
Haskell, Frank A. 74
Hastings, S. D. 18, 24
Hatch, Edward 69
Hatcher's Run, VA
  Battle of 35, 39, 75, 76, 77
Hauser, John F. 39
Hawley, William 36
Hayes, Samuel 99
Haynes' bluff, MS
  Battle of 44
Hayward, Frank A. 76
Hearsey, William E. 99
Heg, Hans C. 50
Helena, AR 65, 66, 86, 89, 98
  Engagement at 65
Helliwell, Albert 101
Helmer, C. D. 12
Hemstead, TX 90
Henderson's Hill, LA
  Battle of 44
Henning, Benjamin S. 90
Henry, William J. 49
Hernando, MS 71
  Skirmish at 47
Hernando Road, TN
  Skirmish on 77
Herron, Francis Jay 56
Hersberg, Ernst F. 94
Hesse, Gumal 80
Heth, Henry 35
Hibbard, Elisha C. 60
Hicks, Henry A. 101, 102
Hill, Edgar P. 59
Hill, Washington 96
Hillier, Spencer S. 95
Hobart, Harrison C. 57
Holden, MO 83
Holly Springs, MS 54, 69
Honey Springs, Indian Territory
  Battle of 91

116

117

119

Miller, Andrew G. 4
Miller, Jesse S. 46
Miller, W. G. 12
Miller, William H. 89
Milligan, _____ (Colonel) 103
Mills, _____ (Paymaster
        General) 18
Mills, Simeon 10
Milwaukee 62, 64, 65
Milwaukee Free Democrat 3
Milwaukee Regiment 60
Milwaukee Sentinel 13
Milwaukee Telegraph 1
Milwaukee, WI 3, 9, 10, 12, 13,
        20, 21, 27, 28, 31, 37,
        45, 46, 60, 73, 77, 78,
        79, 81, 82, 89, 92, 93,
        99, 100, 106
Mine Run, VA 85
  Campaign 40
Minnehaha (steamer) 19
Missionary Ridge, TN
  Battle of 34, 46, 51, 57, 61,
        63, 98, 100
Missionary ridge, TN
  Battle of 54
Mississippi Regiments
  Infantry
    16th Regiment 43
Mississippi River 29, 44, 66
Missouri Compromise 5–6
Missouri Regiments
  Artillery
    1st Battery 104
  Cavalry
    4th Regiment 92
Mitchell, Henry A. 34
Mitchell, Ormsby MacKnight 45
Mitchellville, KY 57
Mobile & Ohio Railroad 69
Mobile, AL 38, 50, 56, 60, 64,
        65, 67
Monitor, USS 96
Monroe, WI 97

Monroe's Crossing or Cross
        Roads, SC
  Engagement at 103
Montevallo, MO 90
Montgomery, AL 72
Montgomery, Milton 61
Moore, Jonathan B. 70, 71
Moore, Webster P. 36
Moorefield, WV
  Engagement at 104
Moore's plantation, LA
  Engagement at 72
Morgan, George W. 93
Morgan, John Hunt 50
Morganza, LA 56, 60, 73
Moscow, TN 66, 71, 84
Mossy Creek, TN 87
Motley's Ford, TN 87
Mound City, WI 19
Mount Elba, AR 65
Mount Vernon, KY 95
Mouse Creek, TN 107
Mulberry Mountains 91
Mulligan, James Adelbert 103
Munfordville, KY 106
Murfreesboro, TN 29, 50, 57, 61,
        68, 95, 97, 100, 102
Murphy, Robert C. 44
Murray, Edward D. 58

N

Nansemond River 94
Nashville & Chattanooga Railroad 68
Nashville, TN 54, 57, 58, 61, 68,
        72, 79, 80, 87, 88, 94, 95,
        97, 98, 100, 102, 107
  Battle of 44, 48, 50, 61
Nasmith, Samuel J. 61
Natchez, MS 49, 71
Neosho Valley, KS 81
New Berne, NC 54, 55
New Creek, WV 103, 104
New Lisbon, WI 102
New Madrid, MO 97, 98, 99

Battle of the Crater 75, 76, 77
  Siege of 35, 38
Petersburg, WV 103
Pettibone, Augustus H. 56
Philadelphia, PA 30
Philbrook, Alva 60
Philippi, WV 104
Pickard, J. L. 24
Pier, Colwert K. 76
Pierce, Guy C. 37
Pile, William A. 104
Pine Bluff, AR 64, 65
Pine Knob, GA
  Battle of 36
Pinkney, Bertine 36, 56
Pinney, Oscar F. 96
Pittsburg Landing, TN 19, 49, 51,
    52, 53, 95, 102
  Battle of 28
Platt, Arthur 46
Pleasant Hill, LA
  Battle of 44, 50
Pleasant Hill Landing, LA
  Battle of 71
Plummer, Philip W. 39
Plunkett, William H. 52
Po River
  Battle of 85
Pocotaligo, SC
  Engagement at 47
Point Lookout, MD 94
Poison Springs, AR
  Battle of 45
Polleys, Ames W. 49
Pomeroy, Henry 86
Pond, James B. 90
Poole, DeWitt C. 47
Pope, John 41, 97
Pors, _____ (Draft
    Commissioner) 22
Port Gibson, MS
  Battle of 46, 53, 59, 66, 93,
    98, 105
Port Hudson, LA 37, 56, 66, 73
Port Scott, KS 90

Porter, Fitz John 84
Portland, OR 2
Portsmouth, VA 94, 96
Potomac River 29, 84, 103
Powers, William P. 95
Prairie d' Ane, AR
  Battle of 64
Prairie du Chien, WI 28, 68
Prairie Grove, AR 44, 45, 56
  Battle of 56, 91
Pratt, Calvin Edward 38
Pratt, David C. 102
Price, John M. 47
Price, Sterling 49, 50, 54, 72, 101
Prince George Court House, VA 96
Pritchard, Benjamin D. 88
Proctor's Creek, VA 96
Proudfit, James K. 47
Pugh, Robert T. 83
Purdy, James T. 94
Purman, D. Gray 78

Q

Quantrill, William C. 91

R

Rabe, Lewis 94
Racine, WI 3, 20, 37, 55,
    58, 68, 70, 93, 94, 95, 97,
    98, 99, 100, 101, 102, 103,
    105, 106, 107
Raleigh, NC 105
Ramsey, Edward A. 37
Ramsey, William H. 24
Randall, Alexander W.
    6, 7, 8, 9, 10, 17, 27
Ransom, Thomas E. G. 49
Rappahannock River 41, 62, 84
Rappahannock Station, VA
  Battle of 38
Rathbun, Charles A. 95
Rawley, Amos O. 55
Ray, W. Augustus 77

123

Battle of 35
Suffolk, VA 94, 96
Sully, Alfred 67
Sully's Indian Expedition 67
Superior, WI 67
Sweet, Alba S. 98
Sweet, Benjamin J. 39, 57
Sweet, Sylvester E. 98
Symes, George G. 79

T

Taberville, MO 90
Taggart, Alfred 82
Tazewell, TN
  Battle of 93
Tennessee Regiments
  Infantry
    60th Regiment 59
Tennessee River 69
Terre Noir, MS
  Battle of 45
Texas Rangers 86
The Star Spangled Banner 7
Thomas A. Scott (steamer) 56
Thomas, George H. 61
Thorne, Gerrit T. 65
Throup, Martin 77
Tigerville, LA 46
Tillson, John 70
Titus, Daniel 97
Torrey, William H. 86
Totopotomy River, VA
  Battle of 74, 85
Totten, Enoch 38
Totten, Joseph Gilbert 56
Trading Post, MO 90
Trenton, TN 99
Tullahoma, TN 80
Tupelo, MS 50, 72
  Battle of 72
Turner, Henry 104
Tuscumbia, AL 45, 102
Tuskegee, AL 72

U

U. S. Supreme Court 4
U. S. Troops
  Artillery
    2nd Regiment 37
Union City, TN 99
United States Sanitary Commission 30
Upper Missouri River 67
Utley, William L. 18, 58

V

Vallee, John F. 95
Van Buren, AR 91
Van Cleve, Horatio P 95
Van Dor, Joseph 41
Van Dorn, Earl 54, 102
Varnell's Station, GA
  Engagement at 87
Vaughn, Samuel K. 55
Vermont Regiments
  Artillery
    1st Light Battery 106
Vicksburg, MS 29, 52, 53, 54, 56,
    59, 62, 66, 69, 71, 72, 89,
    93, 98, 105
  Battle of 44, 49, 54, 59, 93
  Siege of 46, 47, 53, 64, 66,
    71, 89, 105
Vilas, William F. 59
Virgin, Horatio H. 70
Virginia and Tennessee Railroad 104
Virginia Central Railroad 39, 41
Virginia Regiments
  Artillery
    Virginia Battery 93
  Infantry
    48th Regiment 42
Vittam, David S. 90
Vliet, John B. 82
Von Baumbach, Carl 60
von Deutsch, Gustav 15, 92
Von, Fred Baumbach 73
von Schlen, J. C. Her 94

125

Vosburgh, John B. 81

W

Wade, J. T. 2
Wadsworth, _____ 18, 28
Wadsworth, James S. 40
Wagoner, Samuel C. 48
Wait, Joseph W. 94
Waldron, AR 91
Walker, Charles H. 57
Walther, Geo. H. 73
Walther, George H. 73
Wapping Heights, VA
    Battle of 85
Ward, Lyman M. 49
Warner, Clement E. 74
Warner, William 79
Warrensburg, MO 72
Warrenton Pike, VA 35
Warrenton, VA 55, 84
    Battle of 35
Washburn, Cadwallader C. 66
Washburn, Cadwallader C. 16, 89
Washington, DC 16, 27, 29, 32,
    34, 36, 38, 39, 41, 43,
    47, 52, 53, 54, 58, 59,
    62, 63, 69, 70, 75, 76,
    94, 96, 98, 105, 106,
    107
Waterloo, AL 88
Watertown, WI 37
Watrous, Jerome A. 1, 2
Watrous, O J. 1
Watson, W. H. 16, 18
Waupun Times 14
Waupun, WI 10
Waynesboro, GA
    Engagement at 103
Waynesville, MO 82
Webster, Daniel 92, 93
Weehawken, NY 84
Weldon Railroad, VA
    Battle of 43, 77
West Plains, MO 87

West, Francis H. 68
West Point, AL 88
West Point, VA 55, 94, 96
West, Theodore S. 60
Westbend, WI 22
Westinghouse, Levi 95
Westport, MO 101
Wheeler, Henry L. 100
Wheeler, Horace M. 38
Wheeler, John R. 51
Wheeler, Joseph 57, 87
Wheelock, Arthur B. 99
Wheelock, Carlton B. 47
Wheelock, Jesse D. 78
Whipple, Charles 55
Whippy Swamp, SC
    Battle of 52
Whitcomb, W. W. 13
White, Calvert C. 64
White House, VA 76
White, Richard H. 90
White River, AR 65
Whitesburg, AL 54
Whitewater Bridge, MO 87
Whitewater, WI 2
Whiton, Chief Justice 3
Whittaker, Charles 64
Whittlesey, Luther H. 46
Whytock, John 89
Wilderness, VA
    Battle of 35, 38, 40, 42, 85
Williams, Charles H. 59
Williams, John A. 64
Williamsburg, VA 94
    Battle of 38
Wilson, George 50
Wilson, James H. 88
Wilson's Creek, MO 56
Winchester, TN 87
Winchester, VA 36, 39
    Battle of 36
Winkler, Frederick C. 62
Winnsboro, SC
    Capture of 47

CPSIA information can be obtained at www.ICGtesting.com
Printed in the USA
LVOW07s2359081214

417886LV00001B/22/P